HANDLING PROBLEMS OF PEACE AND WAR

HANDLING PROBLEMS OF PEACE AND WAR

An evangelical debate

Edited by Andrew Kirk

John Stott,
Jerram Barrs, Alan Kreider
and others

Marshall Pickering

Marshall Morgan and Scott
Marshall Pickering
3 Beggarwood Lane, Basingstoke, Hants RG23 7LP, UK

Copyright © 1988 Andrew Kirk, John Stott, Jerram Barrs,
Alan Kreider
First published in 1988 by Marshall Morgan and Scott Publications Ltd
Part of the Marshall Pickering Holdings Group
A subsidiary of the Zondervan Corporation

British Library CIP Data
Stott, John,
    Handling problems of peace and war.
    1. Nuclear warfare—Religious aspects—
    Christianity
    I. Title   II. Barrs, Jerram   III. Kreider,
    Alan   IV. Kirk, J. Andrew
    261.8′73   BR115.A85

ISBN 0–551–01553–5

Text set in Linotron Sabon
by Input Typesetting Ltd, London, UK

Printed in Great Britain by
Camelot Press Ltd, Shirley, Southampton

CONTENTS

Part IV TOWARDS A CONSENSUS?

INTRODUCTION

The Christian Church has debated the themes of war and peace, violence and non-violence for an exceedingly long time. They are, of course, perennial issues of great magnitude. As a result of humanity's constant rejection of 'the things that make for peace' (Luke. 19.42), war and violence have now become a tragic part of the human condition. The world, therefore, will continue to suffer all kinds of aggression until the Prince of Peace returns to establish a new kind of world (Rev. 21.4).

For Christians the reality of war and violence can never be merely an intellectual question, to be dealt with, for example, as the subject of some essay which candidates for full-time ministry are expected to write. For one thing the Church has been guilty of its fair share of organised violence. Even after centuries the memory of such shameful actions as the Crusades, the persecution of minority groups (in particular Jews) which did not conform to the beliefs of Christendom, the Inquisition, the forced conversion of the Amerindians of Central and South America, cannot be erased. In recent years we see people proud to be known as Christians involved in sectarian murders in Northern Ireland, directing a brutal police state in South Africa, struggling for supreme power in the Lebanon. We might also mention the countless church leaders who have readily blessed war between nations and oppression against dissidents within a nation. Finally, on the other end of the political spectrum, there are those who have sought to provide a convincing theological rationale for the violence of those who claim to be the vanguard of the workers of the world with the right, in their own eyes, to promote the revolution.

The subject, therefore, is hardly external to the Church. It has been and remains a matter of its internal conscience: what policy should it adopt when faced with situations of acute conflict in which, willy-nilly, it is caught up? As a result of extensive involvement in those myriads of places around the globe where people have suffered as the result of other people's violence – e.g. in Uganda, the refugee camps on the Thailand-Campuchean border, the communal violence in India and Sri Lanka, the brutality metered out to ordinary people in El Salvador, the denial of legitimate aspirations on the West Bank of the Jordan, the irrational racial strife in Western nations – the Church is faced with a series of ethical issues of a political nature, and with deep pastoral concerns. Without any desire to boast, one could compile an impressive list of actions that Christians have taken, as a conscious response to their beliefs, to forestall, end or minimise situations of violence.

The Christian Church is not, of course, an island to itself. Its members have dual nationality: they are members of the kingdom of God and they are citizens of a particular nation. Christians, therefore have a responsibility, like any other citizen, to decide how they ought to react to their country's defence policy, military alliances and presumed enemies. It is this responsibility, related particularly to the deployment and possible use of nuclear weapons, which has in the last few years especially exercised the minds and consciences of Christians living in the West.

Perhaps, more than anything else, the decision in the late 1970s and early 1980s by a number of European nations in NATO to allow a new generation of nuclear warheads on their soil (notably Cruise and Pershing missiles) has led to a vigorous renewal of the moral and strategic arguments for and against the deployment and possible first use of such deadly, destructive weapons. In recent years there has been in Britain a resurgence of the Campaign for Nuclear Disarmament, and the incredible saga of the women of Greenham Common, in Holland the massive peace movement, in West Germany, aggressive anti-nuclear demonstrations, in Spain the emotive referendum on continuing involvement in NATO, in North America the Roman Catholic bishops' pastoral letter on the nuclear question; also the Report of the Palme Commission, the Church of England's General Synod's debate on 'the Church and the Bomb', the Stockholm disarmament and verification treaties, the meetings of Gorbachev and Reagan in Geneva and Reykjavik, and Washington and other notable activities. It is hardly surprising that all this has been accompanied by a spate of publications on the nuclear issue, not least from the pens of Christians (see bibliography).

In 1982, only a few months after it was born, the London Institute for Contemporary Christianity, together with the Shaftesbury Project for Christian social involvement, initiated a process of study and reflection with the aim of adding its own grain of sand to the debate. Both bodies are committed to the pursuit of Christian thought and action from within a framework provided by the whole message of the Bible. They also both work on the principle of bringing biblically-minded Christians together to hammer out whatever differences they may have concerning the interpretation and contemporary application of God's Word, through the Scriptures. The War and Peace project which, as such, began with a weekend conference in October 1982, was consciously designed to further understanding among Christians known not to agree about the nuclear question. One of the main purposes throughout has been to make as much progress as possible towards agreement in a number of areas.

The process has continued, by fits and starts, since that time. In preparation for the original conference three leading exponents of different positions on nuclear warfare were asked to submit a summary of their arguments: Alan Kreider who represents the historic 'Peace Church' commitment to total abstention from war; Jerram Barrs who believes that the implementation of God's justice could require, in certain circumstances, a nuclear first strike, and John Stott who is convinced that the classical just war theory lays down principles for the waging of war which categorically exclude all use of weapons of indiscriminate, mass killing.

Another conference was called the following December (1983). Further papers were commissioned for that meeting and the discussion broadened to include strategic military preoccupations and a look at the notion of the 'enemy'. Two important conclusions emerged. Firstly, biblical Christians disagree among themselves largely because, in deciding on ethical issues, they use the Bible in different ways. Secondly, disagreements are also the result of a variety of views on the Church, the State and Christian involvement in public life.

Participants in the second conference resolved, therefore, that both these matters should be pursued further. In the first place, Jerram Barrs, Alan Kreider and John Stott were asked to make a short explanatory statement of their hermeneutical presuppositions and the methods they used to arrive at their respective positions. Richard Bauckham and Gordon McConville, who had not been involved in the project up to that time, were asked to 'assess' the results, in the sense of reading and commenting critically on each original contributor's self-understanding. All five then met for a session of 'cross-examination' and discussion to clarify the three positions adopted. The 'assessors' then produced a report on the hermeneutical methods, seeking to uncover the fundamental differences of method and assumption which caused the disagreements and how they might be resolved.

In the second place, a small group were asked to give their mind to questions surrounding the Christian's responsibility to the nation-state with a view to breaking fresh ground. They were requested to give special attention to significant historical events which have influenced different churches, to biblical studies on such topics as God and the nations, nationhood, the relation of States to one another, the international responsibilities of national governments, the concept of corporate solidarity and finally the theological and practical question of how Church and State should relate in different political situations (e.g. in democracies, totalitarian regimes, pluralist and unitary cultures). The members of the group, David Atkinson, John Gladwin, Andrew Kirk and Donald Shell, having prepared short position papers touching on some of these issues, met for a long session to suggest pertinent material to be included in a composite document. (They are all too conscious that they were not able to cover all the issues suggested to them.)

We now offer the result of these two processes, in the belief that they make a valuable contribution to what, almost inevitably, will remain a continuing matter of controversy. Some may be inclined to groan when they contemplate the rash of books published recently on nuclear deterrence and the conduct of diplomacy in a nuclear age. The present book does not claim to *cover* new ground. That would be difficult, as the controversy between Christians remains the same and has been extensively reviewed in a number of thoughtful publications. It does, however, profess to *break* new ground, in the sense of covering some of the most important material in a fresh way.

The findings which have come out of the project represent more than another symposium in which individuals independently present their own material for inclusion. They follow a pattern different even from the statements and critical responses on particularly controversial subjects which occasionally are compiled into books. Here, as if responding audibly to the challenges of others, protagonists of alternative views debate with each other. Perhaps the most notable feature of this book is the effort, consciously made, to assess particular approaches both to the biblical text and to modern political and social realities. In this sense the book offers a self-critical appraisal of the different assumptions and methods of argument which lie behind the stances taken. This process is quite deliberate, for it is the conviction of those who planned the project that only by exploring the various starting-points and ways of arguing is there any likelihood of moving closer to a common mind – a goal that should inspire all Christian thought.

In order to complement the process of dialogue and point to possible future tasks we have included a further reflection by Richard Bauckham and Gordon McConville on the joint statement on the Christian in the nation-state, and a concluding reflection by Ernest Lucas, the London Institute's Director of Studies and Roy McCloughry, the Director of the Shaftesbury Project.

All those whose names appear as authors are to be especially thanked. They have spent much time and taken enormous care to present a valuable and readable account of their views. Each has entered into the process of discussion in a spirit of genuine Christian openness: doing all they can to listen to fellow Christians, even when they have sharply disagreed. Each one has stated how rewarding the process has been.

This is the first publication of the results of a study process that the London Institute and Shaftesbury Project have jointly sponsored. It is fitting, therefore, to express deep appreciation to both the Institute and Project staff who have served the project efficiently and graciously and the members of the planning groups (drawn from both organisations) who have played a large part in shaping the agenda for the conferences and also encouraged the publication of these findings. Without the considerable support of all these people the book would not have seen the light of day.

Andrew Kirk, Easter 1987

PART ONE

THREE VIEWS

ADVOCATED

Chapter One

JUSTICE AND PEACE

DEMAND NECESSARY

FORCE

Jerram Barrs

1. Issues between pacifists and non-pacifists

a. The long-standing arguments for Christian pacifism

Down the ages a minority of Christians have concluded that a wholly consistent commitment to the teaching and example of Jesus Christ involves a practical renunciation of all participation in war.

Such a conclusion is arrived at by understanding that Jesus' teaching in the Sermon on the Mount about 'being peacemakers' (Matt. 5.9) requires a refusal to resist evil by the use of physical force (Matt. 5.39).

Not only was this Jesus' express teaching, so argues a pacifist, but also the way of life that Jesus himself demonstrated. His crucifixion at the hands of violent men was the supreme statement of a person willing to suffer violence for the sake of the kingdom of God, rather than inflict it on others (John 18.36).

Those who claim to be disciples of this same Jesus must follow his example. If they are going to represent coherently the reality of the kingdom he inaugurated, they cannot be involved at any time in the use of physical force to restrain evil.

This view, which seems to flow from accepting an almost complete opposition between the teaching of the Old and New Testaments, means that Christians can have no part in fighting a war. It also precludes Christians from taking public office in the State, because the passing of laws, the use of courts to try law-breakers, the existence of a police force, and penalising the guilty all take for granted the need to resist evil, using force.

The pacifist case is defended further by an appeal to a particular view of justice and the way in which human beings are called upon to implement it. Only God's justice is retributive, therefore only he has the authority to pronounce his judgement in ways which might issue in killing or maiming people (Rom. 12.17–21). Human justice has the exclusive function of restoring those who do evil to a position of responsible citizenship in society.

In brief, part of the essence of the gospel of Jesus Christ is the requirement, if necessary, of submitting to the actions of evil people rather than trying to resist them with a force that might damage or kill them.

b. Some of the problems that pacifism raises

To the majority of Christians, advocating a policy of total non-violence in the face of wickedness does seem to display, to say the least, a lack of realism about evil in the world. Moreover, the pacifist position fails to distinguish adequately between different reasons and purposes for the use of force. It seems to reduce all force to the arbitrary use of power, as in the case of totalitarian governments. However, force to restrain wrong-doing is openly accountable to public opinion in a democratic political system.

By tending to interpret the wars which God explicitly enjoined on Israel in the Old Testament period as a reflection of a limited understanding of God's purposes, pacifists fail to do justice to the fact that God's judgement is meant to be carried out through human agents. In this way they make God's judgement on human sin inoperable.

2. The Biblical material

a. The justice of God

God's righteous character is the only absolute basis by which we can distinguish good from evil. As the ruler over all things he will, for he is true to himself, judge every failure to measure up to his standards. We ought to be thankful for the justice and judgement of God for it means that human choices and actions are truly significant, and that there is a final difference between right and wrong.

His judgement undoubtedly sometimes entails the death of people (e.g. the Flood, Sodom and Gommorah, Ananias and Sapphira). If we call this penalty cruel and barbaric, then we have to level this accusation directly against God (e.g. Gen. 9.5–6; Deut. 19.11–13). God prescribed the death penalty both in cases of individual wickedness and in war. In the latter case, war was allowed to Israel in situations of self-defence against an unjust attack and to punish the evil of other nations (Josh. 6.21; 8.1–2; Judg. 6.7). In addition, in the extreme case of tyranny, revolution was sanctioned against the regime in power (2 Kgs. 9–11). We should not be surprised, therefore, that the psalmist says of God that he 'trains my hands for war, my fingers for battle' (Ps. 144.1), ' . . . to inflict vengeance on the nations and punishment on the peoples' (Ps. 149.6–7).

b. Justice on earth

In order that his character as judge be reflected in human society God established good government (Deut. 1.15–17; 17.18–20; 2 Sam. 7.8–16; Ps. 89.1–4; 19–37). It cannot be thought of, therefore, as merely a human invention, an institution of convenience conjured up by the whim of human beings. Indeed, Scripture makes plain the inseparable relationship between divine and human justice in a number of places, e.g. 2 Chr. 19.6–7:

> Consider carefully what you do, because you are not judging for man but for the Lord, who is with you whenever you give a verdict. Now let the fear of the Lord be upon you. Judge carefully, for with the Lord our God there is no injustice or partiality or bribery.

To carry out true justice in human society is to imitate the rule of God, and to fulfil his purpose in establishing government. It is a holy and honourable calling.

God had in mind three main purposes in instituting government for the sake of human well-being. Firstly, the governing authorities are responsible for maintaining justice in the fear of God, according to his law and wisdom (Deut. 16.18–20; Prov. 8.15–16). Secondly, they are under divine obligation to punish justly and impartially disobedience to the law

(Deut. 16.8–13; Prov. 17.15). Thirdly, they are to defend the poor, all those who do not have a proper advocate to keep them safe from oppression and injustice (Ps. 146.7–9; Prov. 31.8–9). In each case God calls human rulers to account for their exercise of the office of 'gods', i.e. his representatives on earth (Ps. 82).

Though punishment in Scripture does have both a rehabilitative and educational function, in order to express fully God's extreme displeasure against those who vilify and violate his just demands it must also take on a retributive function, i.e. make concrete God's just vengeance (Deut. 19.16–21).

c. The place of government according to the New Testament
In the revelation of God's new covenant through Jesus Christ his character does not change (Heb. 13.8; Jas. 1.17). God's mercy, which finds its supreme focus in the salvation Jesus Christ achieved, does not set aside his justice (Rom. 3.26; Matt. 18.6–9). Indeed the salvation won by Jesus Christ is perfect precisely because through it both God's justice and love are satisfied.

Jesus' words 'do not resist an evil person' (Matt. 5.39–48) cannot be applied literally in all situations. Any office-bearer, not only those in the public domain (judges, the police, the military) but also those with a God-given responsibility in family and church life (parents and elders), must resist evil. In fact all Christians are called to the practice of both mercy and justice (Matt. 23.23), and this will sometimes mean the use of force to restrain evildoers.

The cross of Christ is the place of God's triumph over evil forces (Col. 2.15), but it has not eliminated evil completely from the face of the earth in this present age. Hence Christ will himself judge evil in the nations by waging war upon it both now and in his second coming (Ps. 2, 72, 110; Isa. 11.4; Matt. 24.30; 25.31–46; Rev. 2.27; 6.16–17; 19.11–21).

Both Jesus, by quoting Psalm 82 with approval (John 10.35), and Paul (Rom. 12.14—13.10) reaffirm the authority of government. Paul quotes the Old Testament injunction not to exact vengeance for oneself personally (Lev. 19.17). Lest this be understood to mean that just vengeance is of no concern to God in the present age, it is important to note what Paul says next. He insists that God has appointed government, whose just judgement is retributive. Those who take on this work, moreover, are servants of God, doing his work in the world (Rom. 13.1–4). If one studies carefully the following texts, it appears that Christians could be involved both in civil office and in the army (1 Pet. 2.13–17; 1 Tim. 2.2; Acts 13.7–12; 16.37–39; 24.10; 25.8, 10, 11; 10.1, 2, 30–48; Matt. 8.5–13; Mark 2.13–14). We must conclude, then, that to be a policeman, to be in government service, to be a member of a jury or of the armed forces are, for Christians, all works pleasing to God.

Christians, therefore, are called both to be the new community by taking up the cross and following Jesus and to be salt and light in the world, exercising in every sphere mercy and justice (Mic. 6.8; Matt. 23.23) and obeying God rather than human beings (Acts 4.19; 5.29; Rev. 13). The more Christians there are in positions of public responsibility the more likelihood there is of justice being done.

The main differences between Old Testament Israel and the New Testament Church do not lie in active involvement in exercising political power (the same principles apply for both Testaments); rather, the means of punishment within the community of believers has changed (1 Cor. 5.1–5; 2 Cor. 10.3–5) and no nation as such can claim to be the covenant people of God.

3. The calling of governments today

No nation can claim to be the new Israel, yet God calls all the nations and their rulers to account before him (Ps. 82, Prov. 8.4, 15–16, Amos 1—2). All governments still have the same responsibilities before God as they always have had: to recognize the rule of law, to punish the evildoer and commend the good, to mediate for and look after the needy and to protect their citizens against aggression.

This calling of governments to punish evil and to protect people against violent oppression cannot be limited geographically. First this responsibility must be fulfilled at home, and Christians should be working for the practice of justice in their own countries both by example and by bringing influence to bear on the powers that be. But no nation exists in isolation from other nations and the injustice of one government often affects the lives of citizens under the protection of another. In such a case the practice of justice must extend abroad in the legitimate commitment to resist aggression and protect the oppressed.

This commitment leads to the need for armed forces to deter aggression by other nations, just as police forces are needed to deter crime within a nation's boundaries. It also means a readiness to wage war should that sadly become necessary. Wars of defence were approved by God for the people of Israel and because of the reality of evil in the world they are a proper part of the work of justice throughout this age. In addition wars waged in defence of a neighbouring nation (i.e. a nation in need) should be seen as an application of the principle of 'love your neighbour as yourself'. Justice and mercy require governments to be ready to

> Rescue the weak and needy;
> deliver them from the hand of the wicked (Ps. 82.4).

Many agree that the forceful resistance of evil is legitimate, and that therefore it is sometimes right to wage war, so long as war is fought for just causes and in just ways. Some, however, insist that nuclear weapons change the situation completely for they are so indiscriminate in their destructive power. They kill civilians and soldiers alike; they destroy the environment and damage the lives of future generations; how can it be moral to use or even threaten to use weapons which are so horrific? Once one button is pressed this age will be over and civilisation as we know it will be destroyed; what is more, such an all-out war could begin by accident.

Thus, it is argued that all Christians, traditional pacifists and proponents of the just war theory alike, must band together and fight for disarmament, for the removal of nuclear weapons from any part of the world over which we have control, and be prepared to suffer whatever consequences may come from abandoning nuclear deterrence. Our only hope, it is said, is to lay down our weapons and trust in God. We should pray for and work for peace, and concentrate on justice at home. If justice is on our side, then God will vindicate the West without us developing, stockpiling, threatening to use, or actually using weapons of such appalling destruction. All the money spent on defence could be used for the poor, for education, etc.

Prayer rather than defence and deterrence, and more money for the poor, appears to be a very spiritual argument. We certainly should pray for peace and trust God and we ought to be in the vanguard of giving practical help to those who are oppressed; but a false antithesis is created if it is accepted that either of these concerns means no commitment to or no money spent on defence. On most occasions Israel had to trust God and to wage war against their enemies (Exod. 17.8–13). It is not the task of the police or the judge to say to the murderer, 'Go in peace back into society, the State will not punish you – we are leaving retribution and restraint to God' – nor is it the task of those charged with the defence of their citizens or the support of others who need help to lay down their weapons and leave everything to God. Similarly the poor and oppressed sometimes need financial aid and other practical help; at other times they need to be forcefully protected from those who would oppress them, by the application of the rule of law at home, and perhaps by arms abroad.

The central point at issue, though, is this: are nuclear weapons qualitatively different from all other weapons? Would a nuclear war be different in kind from all previous wars?

Nuclear weapons certainly have enormous destructive power, but it should be remembered that 50,000,000 people died in the last war by conventional means. Wars are always horrific. Civilian populations always suffer. Even on the domestic scene as soon as law enforcement agencies are faced by an armed gang or by guerilla movements, it is almost impossible to avoid the involvement of non-combatants. This problem escalates with the seriousness of war and the greater use of force.

In addition, a government and armies must be seen as representatives of the people (even in a totalitarian state like Hitler's Germany, or the Soviet Union): they cannot be separated completely into two camps, so that one concludes, 'We will not defend ourselves against a Hitler, a Stalin, or a Pol Pot because the people of their countries are innocent.'

It does not follow, either, that all-out war with the consequent annihilation of our race would be the inevitable result of a nuclear launch by accident or design, or of a limited exchange of nuclear weapons. Even during war rational decisions are made as to whether the conflict should be escalated. Hitler, who does not seem to have been restrained from action on moral grounds, refrained from using chemical weapons during World War II because the allies had them also. Do we really believe that our governments are so foolish as to engage in all-out nuclear war, a war which by definition no one could win? But, whatever we believe about this, Christians can have confidence in God, and he promises that seedtime and harvest, marriage and family, life as we know it, will continue until the end of the age. This world and the human race will be here until Jesus comes back. It is the Lord himself who will bring this age to a close, not a nuclear holocaust.

Does this mean that I consider limited nuclear war to be a good thing, that it would be acceptable for the superpowers to fight a nuclear war in Europe? Certainly not. The points above were made to answer the fear of inevitable holocaust, not to justify limited nuclear war. This raises a fundamental issue and that is that in the West nuclear arsenals exist for deterrent purposes, not for waging war. Governments in the West have made it clear again and again that their intentions are not to wage war but to deter war. If this were not so, they would have used these weapons long before the Soviet Union caught up with the West in the development of its own arsenal.

With nuclear weapons deterrence becomes a much greater factor than at any previous point in history, for the consequences of waging war would be so horrific. This fact does create a kind of security out of the balance of terror. We might think that this is a poor peace, for true peace is the fruit of the restoration of justice in all relationships, and we are very far from that. However, this poor peace is better than none; and, moreover, the weapons will not go away, nor will the ability to make them vanish. Mutual verifiable disarmament by both sides is obviously desirable as long as it does not threaten the poor peace there is. Meanwhile deterrence is an attempt to come to terms with the world as it is; it arises from the commitment to prevent war. The morality of deterrence must be judged by the intentions of those who possess the weapons, not by their destructive power or by worst case scenarios.

It should be noted, too, that in Scripture the level of force used both by God directly and by his people as his instruments of vengeance, is proportional to the level of evil. The Flood, Sodom and Gommorah and the destruction of the Canaanites are obvious examples of this.

I do not point this out in order to justify genocide today, nor to suggest that any nation is comparable to Israel and could consider itself appointed by God to destroy its enemies totally. I make this point only to show that God himself saw fit to use the level of force necessary to restrain and punish a particular evil. We are responsible in our moment of history so to value the principles of justice and the need to resist and restrain evil that we should be prepared to maintain whatever deterrent force is necessary. To abandon deterrence would not produce peace but might bring even greater injustice on the earth. Our calling is to do what can be done to maintain and increase justice in our own nations and elsewhere. At the same time we know that there will be no perfect justice or perfect peace until Christ himself comes to reign on the earth.

4. A response to criticisms

a. Alan Kreider's objections
Alan Kreider has raised four major objections to my position on war and peace. I will state each and then give a brief answer.
i. *My view that power politics is manifested today in an unreconcilable confrontation between East and West is too simplistic an account of current affairs.* I strongly maintain that it is necessary first to criticise one's own country. I have stressed the crucial importance of justice within nations and the Christian's calling to be salt in society. I have even suggested that revolution could be justified in the face of extreme tyranny.

We must be committed to resisting evil at home, and refuse to fight in any war if our country is the aggressor. We are called always to obey God rather than human beings. However, the fact that our own countries in the West have governments which practice evil at times should not make us view the international situation as being a conflict between two equally wicked powers. Without any doubt the USSR is still one of the greatest tyrannies the world has ever seen. It is hardly sanctified common sense to view the USA or the UK as equally wicked. Alan Kreider argues that patriotism inhibits a Christian from discerning clearly where justice lies, and that consequently there is a qualitative difference between national and international justice. However, the difficulties that patriotism creates must not be used, as is the logic of this argument, to allow tyranny free rein. In the real world there have been (e.g. Hitler's Germany), and are, totalitarian states which in their desire to oppress must be resisted.
ii. *My view that justice is only legal and punitive leads me directly to justify the use of nuclear weapons.* I think the

different branches of justice cannot be separated. My support for nuclear deterrence, however, is not based on a desire to punish in order to obliterate another people. It is motivated by the need to uphold the relational aspect of justice which shows concern for the oppressed now and in the future. The purpose of nuclear possession is the deterrence of oppression not the destruction of ideological opponents.

iii. *My views are based on Old Testament passages which apply only to Israel, whereas Jesus teaches a very different ethic for the Christian.* I do not think, as Alan Kreider argues, that it has been clearly shown that the background to the Sermon on the Mount is Roman occupation and that therefore Jesus is commanding non-resistance to evil on every level. It seems evident in the Sermon itself that Jesus had in mind the way the Pharisees had distorted and set aside Old Testament teaching by their interpretations and additions to the law (cf. Matt. 5.17–20, 21, 27, 31, 33, 38, 43). Jesus' teaching is consistent with Old Testament teaching. We are called to manifest both God's holiness and his love in Christ. This should happen on every level. The one must not be set against the other. Nor must the New Testament be set against the Old. There is no Old Testament Israel as a nation today, but God's concern for justice still stands.

iv. *My interpretation of Romans 12—13 is not supported by the text.* I interpreted Romans 12—13 as forbidding personal vengeance and as upholding the Old Testament view that government is divinely ordained to be God's servant and his instrument of vengeance against the evildoer. Alan argues that the proper background for understanding Romans 13 is not the general Old Testament teaching on the nature of government but rather those Old Testament passages which speak of God using the pagan nations. An example is found in Isaiah 10.5 where Assyria is described by God as 'the rod of my anger', 'the club of my wrath'. In such a passage no positive statement is made about government, for the king of Assyria is clearly condemned by God as unjust because of the way he oppresses other nations. Yet, God uses him to judge Israel for its unfaithfulness. So, Alan argues, Romans 13 must be understood in like manner: Paul sees governments as God's 'clubs against evil' but by such a statement he makes no commendation of government, and it is therefore inappropriate to see Romans 13 as providing a positive Christian view of governing authority or of Christian involvement in government.

It seems to me to be poor exegesis to ignore the wider Old Testament teaching about government in favour of a limited number of passages describing how God judged his people by wicked kings. In the context Paul quotes Old Testament general teaching from the Law and Proverbs about personal vengeance and God's vengeance (Rom. 12.19–20; Deut. 32.35; Prov. 25.21, 22. See also Lev. 19.18). He then goes on to discuss the nature of government using the words '*diakonos*' and '*leiturgos*' for 'servant' of God which his hearers were accustomed to hearing in the context of the ministry of the gospel. His appeal to conscience (Rom. 13.5), respect and honour (v. 7), also indicate a positive understanding of government in line with that found in the Old Testament. The description Paul gives of government is of its general calling to rule under God. The background for this must be the Old Testament teaching about the general calling of governments, not the very specific issue of wicked governments being God's 'rod of anger' against his unrighteous people. It is important to note, as I did earlier, that it is not only the government of Israel that has this general calling to rule under God and by his wisdom and justice, but the governments of all nations (Ps. 82; Prov. 8.4, 15–16).

b. John Stott's objections

John Stott has raised three major objections to my position on war and peace. I will once again state each and then give a brief answer.

i. *I take no account of the fact that the Old Testament forbids the shedding of innocent blood.* However, the passage which is quoted to substantiate the prohibition – I Kings 2.31–3 – refers to peace-time rather than war (cf. 1 Kgs. 2.5–6). The blood of Abner and Amasa was innocent blood because they were killed in *peace-time*. In fact in the Old Testament the solidarity of all in a nation is recognised in such a way that women and children, as well as able-bodied men, were killed in warfare. Certainly, as John Stott argues, the Canaanites and Sodomites were 'decadent', but were the babies decadent as well? Yet they were killed also. Sometimes evil is so great that warfare will mean that non-combatants will be killed. As far as the Old Testament is concerned this was certainly God's view.

ii. *Being conquered by an enemy (however oppressive) is a lesser evil than the slaughter of millions of civilians ('better red than dead').* There are two problems here. First, the intention of possessing nuclear weapons is not to destroy civilians but to *deter* warfare. Secondly, the consequence of being 'red' would also mean the death of millions of civilians. It has already done so elsewhere. We have to resist and deter an existing evil with the weapons at hand. If it could be done with conventional weapons then we must be prepared for that particular cost. However, conventional warfare between NATO and the Warsaw Pact would equally result in the death of millions of civilians.

iii. *Old Testament warfare is sui generis; that is to say God's instruction to Israel cannot be applied to nations existing today.* The Mosaic law *in toto* is also unique; nevertheless I would argue that the principles underlying both the law and warfare should be applied today. The Old Testament is not simply past history. We learn from it how to know God's will today.

5. Approaching the interpretation and application of the Bible

I start from the conviction that the Bible is the revealed, authoritative and inerrant Word of God, and that all people therefore should submit to its teaching.

Further, I believe that Scripture is clear in all its basic teaching, and can therefore be understood in a relatively easy and straightforward manner.

Scripure is not subject to the canons of modern relativistic criticism which approaches Scripture with a set of general assumptions completely alien to Scripture itself. The overall message of the Bible contradicts the view that God is not a personal being, or that he has not acted in history in a way that can be recorded. It refutes the notion that God could not reveal truth to human beings in ordinary propositional language, or that biblical law is so strongly conditioned culturally that it cannot be applied either directly or in principle to our culture today.

Scripture should not be made continually subject to the development of doctrinal understanding in the Church and to the 'spiritual' convictions of modern Christians. Neither has Scripture become almost impossible to understand and apply truly, because, as some people imply, the cultural conditioning which affects us all in our vastly different world today is so all-embracing.

What Scripture does assert is that God is Trinity (the three persons of Father, Son and Spirit), who has made human beings male and female in his image. Language, therefore, contrary to the false views of much modern critical interpretation, must be an adequate medium for God to reveal himself to his prophets and apostles.

Biblical revelation, including Old Testament law, far from being conditioned and reshaped by culture, directly confronts and challenges every culture into which it comes. God's revelation, therefore, is not a pale reflection of arbitrary cultural norms but itself shapes culture. God's Word can be faithfully applied to our moment of history by all who submit humbly to the whole message of Scripture, allowing it consciously to confront their cultural prejudice and personal pride.

Scripture itself teaches that God's revelation in the Old and New Testaments is a fundamental unity. The Old Testament, therefore, is the absolutely essential backdrop for understanding the teaching of the New. As a result the moral teaching of the two Testaments should not be set one against the other, nor should the moral teaching of the New Testament be regarded as having made the law of the Old Testament obsolete (cf. Matt. 5.17–18). Rather, the Old Testament law is to be observed by Christians as it was by Christ.

The basic biblical teachings are the framework against which all doctrinal and ethical ideas must be judged. In other words, wherever a problem arises, the first recourse is to go back to the basic pillars of the faith – the person and character of God, creation, the fall and redemption.

Finally, Scripture applies not only to Christians but to all human beings. However, in seeking to apply biblical law to our culture we have to recognise that people's hearts are hardened against God's purposes (e.g. the Mosaic law of divorce).

Chapter Two

FOLLOWING JESUS

IMPLIES

UNCONDITIONAL

PACIFISM

Alan Kreider

1. The Biblical case for a non-violent approach to life

a. The witness of Jesus himself

Pacifism is a word that is often misunderstood. It should not
be confused with passivism, i.e. doing nothing at all about evil.
Rather it stands for a particular strategy for making peace: one
which seeks to 'overcome evil with good' (Rom. 12.21). It
proposes the principle that physical force should not be used
beyond the point at which it ceases to be an expression of
caring for the enemy.

How can individuals, groups and nations restrain and defeat
evil forces? Between the extreme of remaining wholly inactive
and that of releasing a nuclear holocaust there are many
options. Short of engaging in a war in which human life will
be lost, there are numerous alternative strategies, for example,
prayer, verbal persuasion and protest, systematic non-co-oper-
ation, civil disobedience, and boycott. In limiting the means by
which evil may be resisted, the pacifist Christian has much in
common with other believers who defend the legitimacy of war
in extreme circumstances (on the basis of principles classically
summed up in the theory of the just war). For both the pacifist
and the adherent of the just war find unacceptable the modern

strategic notion of 'total war' in which the lives of non-combatatants are dispensable; both find it necessary – at different points and for somewhat different reasons – to say no for the sake of their faith.

Pacifist Christians base their conviction on the life and teaching of Jesus of Nazareth. All Christians agree that he, and no other person, philosophy or ideology, is 'the Way, the Truth and the Life' (John 14.6). But pacifist Christians are convinced that one cannot fully appreciate the meaning of that statement unless one takes full account of the historical reality in which he carried out his public ministry.

Palestine, in the first century, was a political and military tinder-box.[1] According to the Jewish historian Josephus, the occupying forces of the Roman Empire ruled with a brutal disregard for the cultural and religious sensibilities of the subject nation. As a result, a large proportion of the Jewish people was restive under Roman rule. Some of them, who were later called the Zealots, engaged in a protracted guerrilla campaign against foreign occupation which culminated in the Jewish War of AD 66–70.

Jesus knew all about his nation's enemy. For example, when he was nine years old the Romans put down a revolt just outside his home town of Nazareth, crucifying no less than 2,000 Jews to encourage their survivors to be submissive. From his childhood, therefore, Jesus was aware of the intense feelings among many of his fellow Jews which led them to believe that the only thing the Romans could understand was force. It was military combat, and nothing else, that could free the Jewish nation from foreign domination.

Jesus himslf was almost certainly tempted to interpret his own life's work in this way, i.e. to become another freedom-fighter who would fulfil God's justice by evicting the national enemy at sword-point (Matt. 4.8–10; 26.52–3; John 6.15). He was also no doubt tempted in the opposite directions: to withdraw from any form of commitment to the liberation of and justice for his people in the sphere of public life. Obvious options were available to him. He could follow the Pharisees into the pursuit of legalistic quietism; or he could engage with the Sadducees and Herodians in an attempt to make the best of a bad situation by opportunistically collaborating with Rome.

Resisting violence, compromise and withdrawal, Jesus stayed in the Jewish public arena and pioneered an alternative, non-violent way of being politically relevant. His involvement was rooted in two realities which he announced to his contemporaries. Firstly, God's kingdom of justice, peace and spiritual power was dynamically present in their midst. The new life which it offered overcame fear, and contradicted conventional wisdom that sought security either in religion or military strength. Secondly, the God whom Jesus represented and fully revealed could be trusted far more completely than any earthly father. He could be known intimately as *Abba* (literally, 'daddy'), who cares for his children, protects them, and provides for them. In one's relationship to him there could be no room for fear. 'Do not be afraid, little flock,' Jesus admonished his followers (Luke 12.32). All of their needs would be taken care of as they learned to rely, following a radically different lifestyle from their contemporaries, upon the all-embracing love of the Father.

b. The witness of discipleship
Among the many implications of this new relationship to God, under his caring, parental rule, is the supremely important requirement to love our enemies unconditionally (Matt. 5.44; Luke 6.27). We should note that this, according to Luke's Gospel, is the very first piece of ethical teaching which Jesus gave to his disciples. The enemies about whom Jesus was talking must be understood to embrace not only personal enemies but national ones as well, i.e. the Romans who 'will build an embankment against you and encircle you . . . dash you to the ground, you and the children within your walls . . . [and] leave not one stone on another' (Luke 19.43–4).

The people whom Jesus called to follow him and to love God with all their being were to display a radically different set of commitments from those of the tax-collectors and godless Gentiles, and in particular of their national enemies (Matt. 5.46–7). Like their loving heavenly Father, they were to reach out to hostile strangers, and through loving them were to bring reconciliation and make peace. It is 'peace-makers' and enemy-lovers who are 'children of God' (Matt. 5.9, 43). *Jesus, then, calls his disciples unconditionally to respond with love (not killing) to the one enemy whom his nation was tempted to resist by collective violence.*

To people used to thinking and acting in ways familiar to a world dominated by conventional values, the kind of behaviour which this perfect revelation of the Father demands is intensely threatening. Those who practised Jesus' lifestyle had to be willing to take risks for the sake of God's kingdom (Mark 10.28–30). And this led to division and conflict (Matt. 11.34ff; Luke 12.51) with people who felt comfortable with the values of the Romans, the Jewish legalists or the revolutionaries. Jesus could be very threatening. When justly angry in the presence of the naked oppression of poor people, Jesus resisted evil non-violently: by moral force he removed the corrupt money-changes and animal-dealers from the temple, and he drove out the animals with a whip (John 2.15).

c. The witness of Jesus' death and resurrection

How does God make peace with his enemies? Through the death of his Son on a Roman cross (Rom. 5.10; Eph. 2.14). Thereby God incorporated Israel's national enemies into a new fellowship of faith-filled people who would follow Jesus' way (John 12.52; Acts 10.45). Through Jesus' resurrection and ascension to God's right hand, he became the pioneer who frees human beings from the fear of death which imprisons and incapacitates them (Heb. 2.10–12). As they follow him into freedom, they take up their crosses and walk in the way in which he walked (Mark 8.34; 1 John 2.6).

d. The witness of life in the Spirit

By the Holy Spirit, Jesus continues to live in his followers, gathered together in the new community of God's kingly rule. The new relationship which people, adopted as sons and daughters into God's family, may have with God brings freedom from the fear of all possible threats, including the unknown future (Rom. 8.15, 35; 2 Cor. 3.17). So God's intention for the Church is to be a new society, a body (the Body of Christ), a new nation of reconciled enemies (Col. 3.11). Its members are called, in Christ, through the Holy Spirit, to live an existence which experiences 'the powers of the coming age' (Heb. 6.5) and which thereby contradicts the conventional wisdom of this world. *For three hundred years following Pentecost, the Church expressed this new way of living in the Spirit by teaching and practising the love of enemies. Its leaders forbade the taking of life, in war, in abortion, in gladiatorial games.[2] Their non-violence was a part of the preaching of the gospel and a consequence of conversion to Christ.*

e. A strategy for faithful Christians
This body of Christ's people is called to be a counter-culture. And one essential aspect of its nonconformity to the world is testimony – in word and life – that violence is not an inevitable part of human society. The Church, not the State, is the focus of God's purposes in history; it is his primary agent of change (1 Cor. 1.28; Eph. 3.10; Rev. 12.10–11). The Church is a transnational reality; it is God's international nation (1 Pet. 2.9–12). To it, and not to any nation-state, we owe our highest national loyalties. But Christians have become worldly. We have been insensitive to the mangling which war, by forcing members of the body of Christ – brothers and sisters who belong to the same, one Lord – to slay other members, inflicts on the body. How much pain this causes to the Head! And how anti-missionary war is as well, for it also kills those who are potentially reconciled sisters and brothers.

Christians are, to be sure, commissioned by Christ to participate in secular life. No more than Jesus did do they have the option of withdrawing from the tensions of living in society. But their permeation of the world must not be promiscuous. To change metaphors, as salt they must not lose their saltiness (and the character of salty behaviour in Jesus' teaching is spelled out in the rest of the Sermon on the Mount). Never is the presence of Christians intended to leave the world as it always has been. By acting like Jesus, they will inevitably transform relationships and attitudes around them, and open up vistas upon new ways of Kingdom living.

Christians have a prophetic witness. To individuals we address the call to the way of Christ (which is the way of the cross and thus the way of conflict). To governments we address the call to adopt policies which approximate more than they think possible (on the basis of conventional prudential calculation) to the demands of the kingdom – a justice which brings more than an uneasy cessation of actual hostilities. Christians, with deep compassion and without self-righteousness, must point out to those with authority the inevitably destructive consequences of militarism and the absence of trust.

Finally, Christians should be seeking creatively for new areas of action where they can do concrete things in a distinctive, Christ-like way. Often these will be in places where few others are engaged. Christians, as a minority in most societies (only 11 per cent of the UK populace attends church at least once per week), do not need to do everything in our societies. To us, a creative minority, God gives the opportunity to do new, experimental things that embody the 'lateral thinking' of his kingdom.

Concrete examples that spring to my mind include: the Evangelical Christian who is doing a Ph.D. thesis on Soviet strategic policy and acquiring special expertise on space weaponry; Christians who specialise in mediation and conflict resolution between estranged social groups; a Christian who builds bridges by spending two months annually visiting believers in East Germany; a Christian couple who did extensive non-violence training in the Philippines before the expulsion of Ferdinand Marcos. As the Holy Spirit works among God's people, many other ways will emerge to understand the old order and work for the new.

2. A response to criticisms

a. That I overstress the discontinuity between the Old and New Testaments

This criticism assumes that the way that Christians have traditionally understood the Old Testament is right – that God in the Old Testament approves of war. But will this bear close scrutiny? I think not, for two reasons. First, the form of warfare – the 'holy war' – of which the Old Testament approves is markedly different from modern warfare. As studies of Israel's neighbouring states have indicated, it was also markedly different from other forms of ancient warfare.[3] The warfare of God's people required intentional weakness in anticipation of God's miraculous assistance; it also required the burning of captured weapons and booty. Furthermore, there was the matter of genocide (Deut. 20.1–9, 16–18; Josh. 7.10–15; 11.6). All of these cause difficulties – either practical or moral – for most Christians today.

Second, the form of Old Testament warfare that most closely resembles modern warfare – that fought by kings and their technologically-sophisticated armies – is repeatedly condemned by Old Testament writers. Both Samuel and the later prophets saw it as apostasy (e.g. 1 Sam. 8.11–20; Isa. 31.1). A good example of the cultural captivity of Christian thinking is the way in which Christians sweep aside the forms of counter-cultural warfare of which the Lord approved, and uncritically adopt (purportedly with Old Testament justification) the form of national warfare which the Lord saw as a rejection of himself and an adaptation to the ways of the nations.

But while I find a clear rejection of militarism in the Old Testament, I also find God approving a form of warfare which, while intentionally inferior in numbers and technology, could be exceedingly violent. How do I fit that with my understanding of Jesus and the way of his New Testament followers? In the first place, in the 'holy war' I find themes – for example, a gracious God who expresses his care in practical ways; life by faith in a God whose way can seem imprudent – which are continuous between the Testaments.

In the Old Testament, however, I also find a dynamic quality which looks forward to the coming of the Messiah and the age of the Spirit which he would inaugurate. Therefore, while I find substantial continuity between the Testaments, I find discontinuity as well. In Jesus there is fulfilment, perfect revelation and total authority. Jesus himself commented on this difference, as did other New Testament writers (e.g. Luke 9.35; Rom. 10.4; Heb. 1.1–2). Jesus, the Word incarnate, perfectly demonstrated in human form what the Father is like. His teaching about God's kingdom has unique authority, completing (and even superseding – 'but I say to you') the law and the prophets, and calling us all to repentance.

Jesus' way and teaching are made effective and vindicated by his cross – his work of atonement and victory over the powers – and by his resurrection. Through the outpouring of the Holy Spirit, his disciples, formed into a new non-ethnic, transnational nation, are empowered to live like Jesus and to obey his kingdom teachings.

Jesus' work and witness thus both demand and enable new forms of radical, obedient living. Jesus himself gave two illustrations of this:

i. *Divorce.* In Matthew 19.3–12 Jesus said that, in the law, Moses had permitted divorce because of people's 'hardness of heart' (and no doubt also as a means of restraining an even more exploitative treatment of women). But, because of God's original purpose in creation ('from the beginning it was not so'), Jesus' disciples are to go beyond this into life-long monogamy. Indeed, because of the new age of the kingdom, some of his disciples were called into the legitimate state of singleness (despised by Jewish society).

ii. *Retaliation.* The law had restricted this to equal compensation ('an eye for an eye' (Exod. 21.23–51)), thus greatly curbing violence from the seventy-seven-fold retribution of Lamech (Gen. 4.24). But Jesus takes the matter a step further, forbidding all eye-for-eye retaliation (Matt. 5.39) and commanding the new seventy-seven-fold forgiveness (Matt. 18.22).

b. That I undervalue God's concern for justice
This may be true; it is a matter that my conversations with John Stott and Jerram Barrs have forced me to ponder, for which I am grateful to them. And, as I continue to study the Bible, I am still growing in my understanding.

To begin with, I would like to indicate the area in which I am currently doing new thinking – the definition of 'justice'. God, as both Testaments make clear, is clearly 'concerned for justice'. But what kind of justice? As products of a Western culture, we are socialised to think about justice in ways determined by the Romans – in legal, penal terms. Are we, I have been asking myself, as open to thinking about justice in biblical, Hebraic ways? In the Old Testament, God's liberation of a slave people from oppression was the very basis of justice (Exod. 20.1; Deut. 6.20–5). Indeed, God's saving acts were themselves called his 'justice' (*sedekah*) (e.g. Mic. 6.5). As a result, God could require of his people a lifestyle of compassion, in which they would 'do justice' (*mishpat*), love mercy, and thereby walk humbly with God himself.

It is not surprising, therefore, that the Old Testament law – whose motive clauses are rooted in the Exodus ('you were slaves and I freed you; therefore . . .') – is for a people whose justice will be like that of their Liberator: active for the liberation of the poor, oppressed, marginal people. Quite in keeping with this is the Old Testament's anticipation of the One who will decisively bring 'justice (*mishpat*) to the nations' – the non-violent Servant Messiah (Isa. 42.1–4). Do we root our thinking about justice within the original meaning of the biblical words? Do we focus it pre-eminently on the Servant Jesus?

To orient our thinking in this way, I am convinced, could transform us and our priorities. Dwight Eisenhower was a soldier, not a biblical exegete. But in saying that 'every gun that is made, every warship launched, every rocket fired, signifies, in the final sense, a theft from those who hunger and are not fed, those who are cold and are not clothed' he was close to the perspectives of biblical justice.[4] Could it be that some of us, as we talk about the 'justice' which is effected by the arms race, have become complicit in massive unrecognised injustice?

To say this does not mean that I undervalue the fact that God's justice is at times retributive and distributive as well as liberating and restorative; and I acknowledge that he vindicates his justice by many means, including the punishment which he effects. How, in my pacifism, do I handle that? This would require a major discussion, for which there is not space here. But let me make one point. In drawing ethical conclusions from God's actions, the main question seems to me to concern the agent: who is the proper instrument of God's punitive justice? And what, as God's people, is our particular calling?

In the Old Testament God's rule was often seen as localised, restricted to the people and states of Israel and Judah. Through the law God specified means of attaining his just ends – some distributive (through, for example, the Sabbath and Jubilee regulations), some punitive (through, for example, the death penalty for various crimes, including rebellion against parents). But God also used other means, including the raising up of pagan, persecuting nations who would bring judgement upon his unjust people (e.g. Isa. 10.3–4; Jer. 25.8–9; Hab. 1.6ff).

In the New Testament God's people are freed from the limitations of genes and geography. They are still his agents of redistributive justice (e.g. 2 Cor. 8.14 as an application of Luke 4.18–19). Their work for justice will be through the new social forms of their transnational corporate life, and through their solidarity with the weak and the oppressed. No longer, however, are they his agents of punishment (vengeance): that task belongs to secular governments, pagan and sometimes persecuting though they may be (Rom. 12.19; 13.4). Significantly, in the book of Revelation God's children bear witness to his just rule by word and by martyrdom, but never by taking life (Rev. 12.11; 13.10). Lethal punishment is God's task, and that of the Lamb, smiting the nations with the sword of his word (Rev. 19.15).

c. That I misread Romans 13.1–6
I have found the challenge of re-examining this passage to be one of the greatest benefits of the current conversations. Since the fourth century, most Christian interpreters have thought

that the meaning of this passage was obvious: a) that Christians may be instruments of the lethal violence of God's servant the State; b) that they may do so because Romans 12.19, which forbids Christians to engage in vengeance, does so only to them in their *personal* capacity; c) that this passage applies to international violence (war) as well as domestic justice; d) that this passage is directly transferable to the modern nation-state. We must note that this interpretation has been primarily the product of white, male exegetes in the ecclesiastical traditions which have played a dominant role in 'Christian' Western society. As a result of their interpretation, this text has been, according to one recent commentator, 'perhaps the most influential part of the New Testament on the level of world history'.[5]

But to its first-century Roman readers, this passage would have conveyed a meaning very different from this. These readers – Christians from both Jewish and Gentile backgrounds – were conscious that they had been shaped by Christ Jesus into a new nation. Romans 12 and 13 are both directed to the Roman Christians as a body, which in light of the understandings of ancient political philosophy ('body politic') they would have understood in national terms. Romans 12, just as much as Romans 13, is directed to the group behaviour of the Christians within the social context of their most important political unit – the *church*. And that nation, like the nation of Israel to which Deuteronomy. 32.33 ('Vengeance is mine, I will repay') was addressed is not to avenge itself but to leave that to God's wrath (Rom. 12.19).

Why was it necessary for Paul to make this appeal to non-violence to the believers in Rome? Because they were a community of nonconformists living in turbulent times. Recent researches into Roman history have done much to clarify the setting of the letter.[6] In AD 56, when Paul wrote to the Roman believers, many of them had recently returned to the capital after having been driven from their homes as a result of serious disturbances seven years earlier. As a group the believers were still 'everywhere spoken against' (Acts 28.22). Some of them had evidently been tempted to respond to the pressure of the Roman state by two forms of resistance: violent insubordination to the oppressive government of the emperor, Nero; and tax-refusal. Paul, appealing to the Old Testament image of the pagan Babylonian state as God's 'servant' (Jer. 25.9; 27.6; 43.10), urges the members of God's nation in Rome to submit and to pay taxes. He does not spell out the limits of this submission; Paul does not answer all our questions. But the main thrust of his argument is fascinating. So also are some details. The sword which the state bears (*machaira*), for example, was the symbol of *domestic* justice, not of war against another nation. Furthermore, the 'governing authorities' about which Paul was writing were not a modern nation-state; they were a world-government which, though pagan and persecuting, encompassed the known world and incorporated traditional ethnic and cultural enemies.

Of course, in this, as in all passages, some cultural transposition is necessary as we apply it to our time. But this transposition must not be so free as to reverse the original meaning of the text. In this case, I find it beyond the bounds of sound interpretation to use a text, whose original aim was to admonish Christians to be non-violent towards the then world-government, to allow nation-states in our modern world to compel Christians to engage in violent action towards people (whether Christian or non-Christian) of other nation-states.

d. That I am calling Christians to withdraw from the world

I genuinely do not think I am doing this. My conscious attempt is to call Christians, repeatedly, to participate as fully and vigorously in social structures (including government) as possible without ceasing to be salt (Matt. 5.13).

We must not, however, be less concerned than Jesus was that our salt might 'lose its savour'. Much Christian participation in the structures of our society, it seems to me, has been so compromised ethically as to make no specifically Christian contribution. In our jobs we formulate and carry out policies which are precisely those of secular society: Christian soldiers and Christian bankers have been noted more for their honesty, hard work and clean language than for the way that biblical insights shape our attitudes to the enemy nation or to the forgiveness of debt. We have become worldly. When we decide to step out of line it can be costly. Many of us support Christian gynaecologists who have refused to perform abortions, even though their pro-life stance means that they may not be promoted within their profession. Are they withdrawing from the world?

I advocate two courses of action. First, I urge Christians to participate as agents of kingdom change in every area of society, leaving no area to Satan. Jesus Christ is Lord of all! This may, on occasion, lead to some unconventional forms of involvement. In the area of weaponry, for example, it may lead Christians not to do socially respectable things – such as making instruments of killing – but to do socially suspect things like work with the Campaign Against Arms Trade, which publicises the amount of armaments that the UK sells to Third World countries. Or it may involve Christians in training people in alternative forms of behaviour. Jean and Hildegard Goss-Mayr are Austrian pacifist Christians who, in 1984–1985, travelled throughout the Philippine Islands as guests of the Roman Catholic bishops, training priests and people in techniques of non-violent resistance. The success of 'People Power' is in significant measure a product of their labours. What if Christians would engage themselves with similar imaginativeness in other areas of intractable alienation – Northern Ireland, the Middle East, South Africa – in which violence has been tried, endlessly, and cannot possibly lead to justice and peace?

Second, I urge Christians to engage in prophetic, political witness. Whether in or out of government, we must work for 'truth in the public squares' (Isa. 59.14) in an era that often prefers falsehood and secrecy. Furthermore we must participate in the search for 'middle-axioms', policies which, while falling short of the justice, peace and joy of the kingdom, come closer to a non-violent world than do current policies and structures. In our present context, one such middle-axiom would be a freeze on further development and deployment of nuclear weapons. In a world of massive over-kill in which more is being spent on weapons than the entire national incomes of the poorer half of humanity, such would be a modest step. But, as a middle-axiom, it would be a step in the right direction.

3. *Questions for those advocating the use of lethal force*

My conversations with Jerram Barrs and John Stott have been immensely profitable to me. Repeatedly they have caused me to re-read Bible passages that I thought I had understood and to do a lot of rethinking. I still have, however, a number of queries for them, arising out of their respective positions, which I think need answering, and I include a few samples of them here, I start with the arguments of Jerram Barrs.
i. In your concern for war as an instrument of justice, you seem

to speak primarily about the outbreak of war. What limits do you put on violence in the course of war? Are there, as the just war theory has maintained, immoral means of conducting war? If so, how do you determine what they are, and how do you enforce them in wartime? If not, I fear that when the crunch comes our morality will be determined by the methods of the enemy or by military expediency. Is an ethic that sets no limits in practice not in danger of being self-absolutising? When we are willing by nuclear means to threaten to kill without limits and to destroy the well-being of God's entire created order – and if necessary to *do* these things – in order to vindicate a value (even a value as important as our view of justice), has not that value become an idol?

ii. In presenting your case for God's attribute of justice and in demonstrating that he commanded his people to fight, you draw heavily upon the Old Testament. Do you, however, seriously grapple with what the Old Testament has to say about either justice or war? Do you try to ascertain what the texts actually say, and what they meant in their original settings? I have earlier raised questions about justice; let me turn my attention here to war.

As the form of warfare which the Old Testament justified, the *herem* ('holy war') must be important to you. How do you handle passages such as Deuteronomy 20.16–18 and Joshua 11.11 in which God required his people to commit genocide? How do you apply today the fact that in these wars God institutionalised the numerical and technological inferiority of the Israelite armed forces so that they would have to trust (as in the Exodus) his gracious miracle for their victory (Deut. 20.1–9; Josh. 11.6; cf. Exod. 14.14 etc.)? How do you understand God's denunciation of his people's capitulation to the values of surrounding cultures (becoming 'like all the nations') in choosing a king whose style of government will mean the militarisation of their society (1 Sam. 8.4–20)? What role is there in your thought for the prophets' denunciations of militarism, military technology (chariots) and alliances (Is. 30.1–3; Hos. 10.13–14)? What relevance is there for us in God's raising up pagan, persecuting nations – *unjust nations* (Hab. 1.7) – to be his 'servant' (Jer. 25.9)? I fear lest we are tending to use the Old Testament, not as revelation, but as a justification for what our culture has decided to do on other than biblical grounds.

The following are questions that I would put specifically to John Stott:

i. Your argument appears to be based on passages (e.g. the Old Testament prohibitions of shedding blood and, in the New Testament, Romans 13.1–6) which have to do with domestic justice, not on passages which deal with war or international relations. If this is so, why is it legitimate to apply to inter-state warfare principles which refer to domestic justice? I find a difference of quality as well as scale between the two. In domestic justice an element of even-handedness is possible, for at its best the State will be judicious and impartial. In warfare, however, the State (even with the best of intentions) is a party to the dispute. Moreover, because it is in physical danger, it is likely to lose perspective. Can a State really fight a war judicially? What examples from history would you cite of nations which, when contemplating beginning a war, desisted from doing so because their theologians decided it would be unjust? Or, once the war was in progress, which called a halt to hostilities because the means of fighting – e.g. bombing of civilians in urban centres – had involved the systematic shedding of innocent blood? How often, in your knowledge, have Christians – using your criteria for justice – succeeded in warding off unjust wars or in bringing to a halt wars that have become unjust?

ii. Although I agree with many aspects of your reading of Romans 12—13, I also have some problems with your interpretation. Is it correct, as you seem to assume, that Romans 12 deals with the Christian's personal ethics, whereas Romans 13.1–7 deals with their public ethics? The text does not seem to make this distinction. The word 'body', which Paul uses for the Christians (12.4), may indicate that he viewed the Christians themselves to be a new nation (in the words of Robert M. Grant, the body metaphor is 'primarily and essentially political'); and the 'vengeance is mine' passage from Deuteronomy 32.35 was originally given, not to individuals, but to God's nation.[7] In Romans 12.19–21 Paul, in urging Christians never to take vengeance, is addressing them not individually but nationally, as members of a transnational nation. God, not the believers, will take vengeance. Romans 13.4 shows how he will do so – not through the believers but through the State, which, in the Greek, is called 'an avenger for wrath'. Significantly, Romans 13 does not urge believers to participate in this vengeance, but says that Christians are to be 'subordinate' as God does this through his 'servant'. Vengeance is not the calling of the members of the Christian nation; their calling is overcoming evil with good.

May not those recent scholars be right who understood Paul to be saying that the Roman Christians, who were being tempted to insubordination, should be subordinate to God's 'servant' (a pagan, persecuting world-government) just as the Israelites had been to Assyria and Babylonia in Old Testament times? This may explain why early Christian tradition called Rome Babylon (1 Pet. 5.13; Rev. 18.2, etc.). Thus, while leaving vengeance to God, the Roman believers would demonstrate in their life together new, concrete ways of dealing with evil. This understanding would seem to be consistent both with Jesus' teachings, with the epistles which present a vision of the Church as God's new society, and with the book of Revelation.

Finally, for both Jerram and John, I have one basic question – a question that is both historical and hermeneutical – that I do not believe that either deals with adequately. Do you do justice to the original meanings of the passages that we are discussing? To cite one specific instance, do you interpret the teaching and mission of Jesus in the light of the highly specific historical situation in which he lived? In view of what I understand to be the political setting of his life and ministry, I find your limitation of Jesus' teaching on love for the enemy to private, inter-personal relationships to be unconvincing. And this seems to me to be of ultimate importance – because of who Jesus was. As the final, perfect revelation of the Father, his specific teaching and ministry must be the determining norm not only of our personal ethical action, but also of all our ethical stances in the public arena. Ultimately, our understanding of and response to the meaning of world history will be a reflection of our understanding of him.

4. Approaching the interpretation and application of the Bible

a. The authority of Scripture
Both the Old and New Testaments are God's written Word. They are authoritative, therefore, for the faith and life of Christian believers.

Both Testaments contain good news of life and liberation.

This calls us to repentance, new patterns of life and thought, and risky steps of obedience.

The Bible (on the principle of *Sola Scriptura*) is our norm, not creeds or systematic theologies, not natural revelation or cultural or religious tradition.

b. The self-awareness of the interpreter

We must strive to understand and acknowledge our identity and assumptions, whether they be confessional, sociological, political, economic or gender, both before and while we study the Bible. We should adopt a spirit of humble willingness to let God's Word be 'living and active' (Heb. 4.12) in calling us to *new* understandings and *new* acts of repentance, worship and obedience.

Interpretation is not a matter of private opinion or private revelation; it is the work of the whole Church.

c. Exegesis: what the text meant to its first authors and first audience

To ascertain the original meaning of any text we need to proceed carefully through a series of stages. The following steps are indispensable to a faithful understanding of what the authors intended to convey by what they wrote:

i. As far as possible, establish the actual text the original author wrote.

ii. As certain the original meaning of words and literary forms (linguistic analysis).

iii. Ascertain the relationship of the text to the rest of the passage and to the rest of the work of the author (literary analysis).

iv. Discover the historical context of the writing by gaining as much reliable information as possible from contemporary documents: for the Old Testament Akkadian, Assyrian and Babylonian materials, for example; for the New Testament the Qumran documents, Josephus, apocryphal writings, rabbinic writings, pagan classics and the early Fathers.

v. Relate the text to the rest of the Bible, avoiding a selective use of biblical evidence, seeking the witness of the whole Bible on any given subject, dealing with any apparent differences which emerge by reconciling as far as possible, without forcing unnatural meanings on the text, the seeming discrepancies.

vi. Recognise the implications which follow from the Bible

being about history. It is not a repository of sacred texts from which we can draw at random; rather, it is supremely a record of 'salvation history' in which God is acting to redeem humankind. As a result of the historical nature of God's revelation, his will is not fulfilled in exactly the same way in every situation.

d. Jesus Christ as our hermeneutical key

The Old Testament speaks of God's *promises*. It is a record of God's gracious acts of creation, liberation, covenant-making, and law-giving. It enunciates basic theological themes which permeate both Testaments. It shows that the historical direction of God's saving purposes are towards the inclusion of men and women from all nations in the community of his people and towards the restoration of the *shalom* (wholeness) of all creation. The Old Testament, however, is incomplete. It anticipates the coming of the Messiah, who will bring a deeper liberation and a more complete revelation.

The New Testament speaks of *fulfilment*. Christianity is by definition a messianic faith. Jesus Christ is the centre of the entire Bible. He is the incarnate Son who shows us the Father. He is the authoritative teacher of God's truth, and the one and only atoning sacrifice for the sin of the whole world. Through his resurrection he is the victor over the powers. He breathes the Holy Spirit upon all his disciples and brings outsiders/ enemies (Gentiles) into a new non-ethnic nation spread among all nations. He proclaims and brings to fruition God's kingdom which represents the new era of salvation history.

Jesus Christ is, thus, the hermeneutical key to both Testaments. As far as the Old Testament is concerned, Jesus exhibited sensitivity to historical sequence. In Matthew 19.3–12, for example, he asserted that God's creational intent (prior to the Fall) takes precedence over Old Testament laws which God had given 'for the hardness of your heart'. He also points to the transforming presence of God's kingdom, in which God will do new things. Throughout his ministry Jesus demonstrated moral insight, revealing God's true purposes and the intention which underlay Old Testament legislation. Jesus' own hermeneutical method must be authoritative for us. As far as the New Testament is concerned, the identity of the writers is significant: they are people who had taken the dangerous step of becoming disciples of their Master, Jesus. The purpose of these writers was thus to pass on his way, his truth, his life, applying these to the situations of the congregations which comprised the cells of the movement which he had founded. The point, for the early Christians, was to be like Jesus. In their individual and corporate lives they sought to imitate and exemplify his approach to conflict and service (Eph. 4.13; 1 John 2.6).

The New Testament fulfils and transforms Old Testament themes. For example, the Old Testament holy war (Hebrew *herem*; in the Septuagint Greek translation *anathema*), which served to preserve the holiness of God's nation (Deut. 20.18), has been transformed by the New Testament writers into church discipline (*anathema*), which seeks to preserve the purity of God's transnational nation by redeeming the offender.

e. Application: what the text means here and now

We need, first of all, to recognise the historical distance that exists between the text and the late twentieth century (e.g. between the world government of the first century and the nation-states of today). Second, we must allow the text to function negatively by providing us with the critical criteria to judge the ideologies, social mores and unexamined assumptions which dominate our own societies. Third, we must also allow the text to function positively by actualising in contemporary situations the life which Jesus lived (and the disciples of the early Church who imitated him and passed on his life). *Living now as they lived then* will take on somewhat different forms in various societies (totalitarian, democratic, 'Christendom'). It will require Spirit-guided discernment by the community of God's people as we seek to apply the Bible to our situation.

As we use the biblical text today, our main guiding principles will be:

i. Look for a deep commonality between major theological themes and specific events, between moral imperatives and occasional counsel. Where there is apparent tension between two passages, look for fresh light on both of them, and re-examine the preconceptions which we bring to the text.

ii. When the Bible does not speak directly on an issue (e.g. the killing involved in abortion) we should make a careful use of analogy, making sure that the analogies are based on biblical perspectives and not those of our milieu.

iii. Be suspicious of anything that does not look or sound like Jesus.

iv. Be suspicious of anything that does not call us to move beyond where we are into new areas of understanding, trust, obedience, and liberated living.

v. Expect the Holy Spirit to make the biblical passages live in our lives, taking us into uncharted territory where faith is necessary in order to live.

Notes

1. Margin Hengel, *Victory over Violence* (SPCK, 1975), p. 56; Richard J. Cassidy, *Jesus, Politics and Society* (Orbis Books, 1978).

2. Jean-Michel Hornus, *It Is Not Lawful for Me to Fight: Early Christian Attitudes toward War, Violence and the State* (Herald Press, 1980); Michael J. Gorman, *Abortion and the Early Church* (Inter Varsity Press [US], 1982).

3. Millard J. Lind, *Yahweh is a Warrior: the Theology of Warfare in Ancient Israel* (Herald Press, 1980).

4. Address, 'The Chance for Peace', before the American Society of Newspaper Editors, 10 April 1953.

5. Ernst Bammel, 'Romans 13', in E. Bammel and C.F.D. Moule (eds.) *Jesus and the Politics of His Day* (Cambridge University Press, 1984), p. 365.

6. J. Friedrich, W. Pöhlmann, and P. Stuhlmacher, 'Zur historischen Situation und Intention von Rom. 13.1–7'. *Zeitschrift für Theologie und Kirche*, 73 (1976), pp. 131–66.

7. Robert M. Grant, *Early Christianity and Society* (Collins, 1978), p. 36.

Chapter Three

NUCLEAR WEAPONS CHANGE THE POSSIBILITY OF WAR

John Stott

Introduction

The Christian case for nuclear pacifism which I want to argue is moral, not political, although of course it has political consequences. As William Temple used to insist, the contribution which we have to make as Christians lies in the field of principles, not policies. The development of policies and programmes is the responsibility of specialists. Our Christian faith as such is no substitute for expertise. So the case for nuclear pacifism relates not to disarmament policies, but to the prior question of principle, namely whether it could ever be morally justified to use nuclear weapons.

The case for nuclear pacifism bridges the divide between Christian pacifists and Christian adherents of the just war tradition. It is obvious that all total pacifists are nuclear pacifists too. It is not always recognised, however, that many defenders of the just war theory limit its application to wars fought with conventional weapons and declare that in regard to nuclear (and other indiscriminate) weapons they belong to the pacifist camp.

1. *The essence of the case for nuclear (relative) pacifism*

According to the just war theory (first propounded by Greek philosophers, but later elaborated by Christian theologians), (a) the force used to resist and/or punish evil must be strictly *controlled*, (b) the suffering caused by war must be *proportionate* (i.e. proportionately less than the suffering endured if war is avoided) and (c) the destruction involved, especially of human life, must be *discriminate* (i.e. limited to military targets, while guaranteeing immunity to non-combatants).

These three adjectives ('controlled', 'proportionate' and 'discriminate') are all integral to the just war theory. They are all also inapplicable to a nuclear war, whose effects would be uncontrolled, disproportionate and indiscriminate. Therefore a nuclear war could never be a just war, and the use of nuclear weapons must be renounced as immoral. The argument is not that the invention of nuclear weapons has altered God's concern for justice, but that it has a bearing on how God's justice is administered. God does not seek or secure a just goal by the use of unjust means.

The conviction that a nuclear war could not be a just war, because it would infringe basic principles of the just war theory, is widely held. The use of weapons of indiscriminate destruction has been condemned by the Roman Catholic Church at the Second Vatican Council (1965), by the British Council of Churches (1980), by the General Assembly of the United Nations (1981) and by the 'Life and Peace' ecumenical conference at Uppsala (1983).

2. *The biblical basis for nuclear (relative) pacifism*

The case for nuclear pacifism is consistent with centuries of Christian tradition, and should not therefore be lightly set aside. Nevertheless, Scripture rather than tradition, which is no more than the church's understanding of Scripture, is our final court of appeal. I would cite two main lines of biblical evidence for the case, the first relating mainly to the Old Testament, and the second to the New.

a. The biblical (especially Old Testament) prohibiton of
shedding innocent blood
The importance of 'blood' in the Bible is that it is the carrier,
and therefore the symbol, of life (whether animal or human).
Thus, 'the life of a creature is in the blood' (Lev. 17:11), and
'the blood is the life' (Deut. 12:23). In particular, human blood
is the symbol of human life: the reason why it is sacrosanct is
that it represents the life of human beings who have been made
in God's image (Gen. 9:6). Consequently, to shed blood is to
take life by violent means (i.e. to kill), while to shed innocent
blood is to take innocent human life, which is strictly forbidden.

The main exception to the prohibition of shedding human
blood relates to the execution of murderers. In their case,
'whoever sheds the blood of man, by man shall his blood be
shed' (Gen. 9:6). As a judicial act, its purpose was to show not
that human life was cheap (by taking away the murderer's) but
that it was precious (by avenging the victim's). This does not
mean that capital punishment was in all circumstances manda-
tory, for the first murderer's life was spared and protected
by God (Gen. 4:13–15), but in terms of retributive justice it
indicated what the murderer deserved. If the execution took
place, it was to be regarded not as another murder (a further
shedding of innocent blood) but as the divinely permitted
penalty for murder (the shedding of guilty blood, i.e. the blood
of the guilty).

One of the gravest of all offences, according to the Old
Testament, was the shedding of innocent blood, the wanton
killing of human beings bearing God's image. Hence the
provision of the six cities of refuge, three on each side of the
River Jordan. They expressed the difference between murder
(intentional) and manslaughter (accidental), provided protection of the manslayer from the avenger of blood, and so put a
stop to blood feuds. According to the prophets, the two greatest
sins of God's people, on account of which his judgement would
fall upon them, were 'idols' and 'blood', that is, idolatry and
murder (e.g. Jer. 7.5–7; 19.4; Ezek. 22.1–4; 36.18). In our duty
to God, nothing is graver than idolatry; in our duty to our
neighbour nothing is graver than the shedding of innocent
blood, whether by an individual (murder) or by an oppressive
regime (arbitrary killings). 'Hands that shed innocent blood'
are among the things God is said to hate (Prov. 6:16f.).

In a nuclear war, millions of civilians would be killed,

meaning that much innocent blood would be shed. The biblical prohibition makes such a prospect intolerable to the Christian conscience.

b. The biblical (especially New Testament) restriction on the power of the state
The passage Romans 12:17 to 13:7 appears, at first sight, to contain an inner contradiction. According to the end of Romans 12 Paul insists, echoing Jesus in the Sermon on the Mount, that we are not to repay evil, but rather love and serve our enemy, and overcome evil with good. According to the beginning of Romans 13, however, Paul affirms, echoing Old Testament teaching, that the State is God's agent to punish evildoers. Thus the first paragraph forbids the avenging of evil, while the second requires it at the hand of the State.

The possibility of harmonisation emerges when it is seen that the anomaly not only exists between the two paragraphs but is actually embedded within the first. 'Do not repay evil for evil ... I will repay', and 'do not take revenge; vengeance is mine' (Rom. 12.17–19). In other words, the reason why retribution is forbidden is not because it is wrong in itself (it is what evil deserves), but because it is God's prerogative not ours, and he exercises it through the State. The two strands of teaching are complementary, therefore. They are not two standards of morality, but two distinct social roles. As private individuals our duty is never to take revenge, but to love and serve our enemy. But as state officials, for example in the police or the judiciary, it may be our duty to arrest a criminal, bring him to justice, try, sentence and punish him.

In its punishing role, however, the State's powers must be strictly limited. Its use of force must be both discriminate (limited to evildoers – criminals within and, by legitimate extrapolation, aggressors without) and controlled (limited to 'minimum necessary force', i.e. what is essential for the purpose of restraining and punishing evil), whether through the police or the army. These two limitations of force (only against evildoers and only what is necessary to resist their evil) are implicit in the text of Romans 13.

c. An interim conclusion
The State may use force, but only discriminately – in the case of the police to arrest and punish criminals, in the case of the

army to engage in a just war by just means for a just end. In both cases, because of the built-in limitations, the State must ensure the immunity of the innocent – of law-abiding citizens in peace-time and of civilians in war-time. The force permitted to the State does not extend to the shedding of innocent blood. Therefore the Christian conscience, which has been schooled by Scripture, must condemn every use of force by the state which is uncontrolled or indiscriminate.

The principle of discrimination, in relation to war, applies in two ways. First, it condemns the indiscriminate use of conventional weapons; for example the 'obliteration' or 'saturation' bombing of certain German cities during the Second World War. Secondly, it condemns all use of indiscriminate (atomic, biological and chemical – ABC) weapons.

3. A response to general objections to nuclear pacifism

a. From the position of those who believe that nuclear war could be a just war

i. *'There are biblical precedents for indiscriminate divine judgement.'* The analogy is inexact, however. Neither the Flood nor the destruction of Sodom was an indiscriminate judgement, since in the former case Noah and his family, and in the latter Lot and his family, were saved. As for the Canaanites, the requirement of their universal destruction was due to their universal corruption. 'The sin of the Amorites' had 'reached its full measure' (Gen. 15:16). Their practices were so disgusting that the land itself had 'vomited out its inhabitants' (Lev. 18:24f.). There is no parallel between those decadent Canaanites and the millions of devout Russian Orthodox peasants, even when the evil tyranny of the Soviet system is taken into account.

ii. *'The distinction between combatants and non-combatants is obsolete.'* Objectors concede that the distinction has a long history, and that it was further defined in the Geneva Convention (1949) 'relative to the protection of civilian persons in time of war'. In modern warfare, however, the argument runs, 'there are no non-combatants. The whole population is sucked into the war effort. Every taxpayer is helping to finance it. Every citizen who works in a civilian job is thereby releasing somebody else for military services.'

In response, we have to agree that modern war tends to be

'total war', and that the old clearcut distinction between a country's small professional army and its population as a whole has been blurred. Nevertheless, we must insist that at least some sections of the community (e.g. the elderly, the physically and mentally sick and little children) have a right to be regarded as 'non-combatants' and therefore immune. To kill such in a nuclear holocaust would be an unacceptable case of 'shedding innocent blood'.

iii. *'Not all nuclear weapons are indiscriminate.'* In the Dulles era of the 1950s the policy was one of 'massive retaliation'. But in the 1960s under Robert McNamara this was succeeded by the strategy of 'counterforce', which limited retaliation to military targets, not cities. And now the key words are 'flexible' or 'graduated' response, while 'tactical' or 'theatre' (as opposed to 'strategic') weapons have become so sophisticated that they can strike a target with an extraordinary degree of accuracy. All this is true. Both changing strategy and the miniaturisation of weapons have made the concept of a nuclear war less indiscriminate. Nevertheless, even the smallest nuclear device causes some radioactive fallout. And, above all, there is the grave risk of escalation once the nuclear threshold or 'firebreak' has been crossed. The notice of a 'limited exchange' is, to say the least, exceedingly dangerous.

b. From the position of pacifism

'If the use of nuclear weapons would be immoral, their possession is equally immoral. The deterrent itself should therefore be renounced.' Certainly moral theologians argue that the intention to do evil is as immoral as the intended evil itself, or that threats are as bad as deeds. But 'possession' is not necessarily 'intention', let alone 'threat'. Indeed, the real intention behind the possession of nuclear weapons is not to use them, but the reverse, to prevent their use. 'Deterrent' is an accurate word. Therefore we cannot declare 'possession' and 'use' to be equally evil.

c. Conclusion

I find myself in the personal dilemma of being both a nuclear pacifist and nevertheless, believing in multilateralist approach to nuclear disarmament. Christian morality leads me to say that the use of nuclear weapons would be immoral, but Christian realism leads me to defend their conditional possession.

Unilateralism (at least the kind which advocates the immediate, total dismantling of our nuclear arsenal) might well make nuclear war more likely. In that case the renunciation of one perceived evil (nuclear weaponry) would cause an even greater evil (nuclear holocaust). Therefore, the urgent search for balanced, multilateral and verifiable disarmament, together with what Pope John Paul II has called 'audacious gestures of peace' (i.e. unilateral gestures intended to break the log jam), seems a more prudent, and in this case a more moral, stance than unilateralism.

I am painfully aware that this stance, which could be epitomised as 'immoral to use, prudent to keep', is a pradoxical position, which appears to some to contain both a logical inconsistency and a practical flaw. The illogicality lies in continuing to keep weapons whose use we say would be evil. The practical flaw is that to forswear use would to some extent undermine the credibility of the deterrent. Not altogether, however, if the other side is kept in uncertainty about use. I can see no way out of this dilemma. Not to declare use immoral would itself be immoral. So, it seems to me, would total unilateral disarmament, since it would be more likely to precipitate than to deter a nuclear conflict. So the dilemma remains. At least our Christian sense of outrage and horror at the thought of using nuclear weapons should stimulate us both to regard their continued retention as permissible only if temporary and to urge our leaders to redouble their efforts to find a safe way to the multilateral dismantling of the world's nuclear stockpiles.

4. A response to particular criticisms

a. In my use of Scripture I am said to take insufficient account of its original setting, and/or to extrapolate too freely
My general response to this criticism, before I come to the two particular biblical arguments I have deployed (the prohibition of shedding innocent blood and the God-given duty of the State), is to agree with the need to pay attention to the original contexts of God's Word. For God always spoke in precise cultural contexts, and his Word cannot be understood in isolation from them. At the same time, God intends his Word to apply to our own contemporary cultural contexts too. Therefore the practice of 'cultural transposition' is an indispensable

hermeneutical task. It involves first identifying the essence of what God has spoken in the text, in its original cultural context, and then transposing it (without falsifying its meaning) to our own contemporary cultural context.

b. The biblical prohibition of shedding innocent blood.
It is asserted by my critics that the biblical references to the shedding of innocent blood are all to domestic, not to international, situations. They condemn murder, not the killing of civilians in war. This is not so, however, and I do not think Scripture justifies this distinction. The principle is stated in the most general way. Human blood is sacred because it represents the life of human beings made in God's image (Gen. 9:6). Therefore, innocent human blood must never be shed. Human blood may be shed only when it is 'guilty' and when specific divine authorisation is given. In the Old Testament there were two such authorisations. The first was the judicial execution of murderers (and of a few other serious offenders); the second was the prosecution of a divinely sanctioned war (e.g. the destruction of the Canaanites). David's general, Joab, was rebuked for 'avenging in time of peace blood which had been shed in war' (1 Kings 2:5, 31–3). In other words, he had presumed to transfer to peacetime a permission which had been granted only for wartime.

To sum up, human blood is sacred. It may never be shed if it is 'innocent'. Specific divine warrant is needed to declare it 'guilty' and then to permit its shedding, whether in capital punishment or in war.
ii. The biblical restriction on the power of the State I have received two criticisms of my use of Romans 12:17—13:7.
a. Paul is not addressing Roman rulers, it is said, but Christian citizens tempted to take up arms against them. Further, what Paul is urging on his readers is non-violent subordination to the State, not participation in government. It is post-Constantinian theologians who have perverted Romans 13:1–7 into an instruction for rulers.

I think this is another false distinction. It is true that Paul's primary aim is to give instruction in Christian citizenship (submitting to rulers, obeying laws, paying taxes etc.). But his teaching *to* believers rests on his teaching *about* rulers. Three times he affirms that their 'authority' has been 'established' or 'instituted' by God (Rom. 13.1, 2), and three times he describes them as God's 'servants' (Rom. 13.4, 6). I cannot find any suggestion in the text that this is a grudging acquiescence in the existence of the State, or that Paul is calling the State 'God's servant' only in the very limited sense that pagan emperors like Nebuchadnezzar and Cyrus were said in the Old Testament to be God's 'servants'. In their case God said he had raised them up for particular *ad hoc* tasks of judging or saving his people. In the case of the State, however, Paul is writing of an established order designed by God for the welfare of society, namely for the promotion of good and the punishment of evil. True, Rome was a tyrannical power; yet Paul declared its authority and ministry to be divine. Was it not in consequence of this belief that he himself on several occasions appealed to Roman justice? So then, although he was laying down the Christian's duty in relation to the State, he was also laying down the State's duty in relation to society.

ii. As with the prohibition of shedding innocent blood, it is claimed, so with the State's authority in Romans 13, the perspective is domestic, not international. and the 'sword' the State bears (verse 4), as the symbol of its authority, is *machaira*, the short sword used for the administration of justice rather than for the conduct of war.

Once again it seems to me that an unwarranted distinction is being made. Take the sword first. It is true that *machaira* was used in executions (e.g. Acts 12.2), but it was also used by soldiers in war (e.g. Exod. 17.13; Deut. 13.15; 1 Chron. 21.5). The point is that it was a symbol of the State's power to take life, without specifying the circumstances in which this might be justified.

As for the State's God-given authority to promote good and punish evil (Rom 13.4), it is true that the primary application of this text is to the preservation of justice and peace in the community. But the defence and welfare of citizens was entrusted to the Roman legionaries. They were soldiers with police duties; there was no separate police force in those days. So their duty to keep the peace included the protection of the people from criminals and aggressors not only within the Empire but also from beyond its borders. I think Paul's readers would have regarded it as natural to make this extrapolation and arbitrary to exclude it.

Of course the judicial processes of the State are dispassionate and orderly (arrest, trial, verdict, sentence, punishment), and war is neither dispassionate nor orderly. Nevertheless, war can be justified if it can be regarded as an expression of retributive justice.

5. *Approaching the interpretation and application of the Bible*

a. The whole Bible

I begin with the conviction that *all* Scripture, being God-breathed, is indispensable to help us believe and live rightly (2 Tim. 3.16). Therefore we have to base our position on Scripture as a whole, avoiding arbitrary selectivity. Alan Kreider begins with the Sermon on the Mount, Jerram Barrs and I with justice and the State. Each side needs to say how it interprets the Scriptures which the other side emphasises. I think it is fair to say that, whereas Jerram and I fully accept the teaching of the Sermon on the Mount as governing our conduct as Christians, Alan does not seem able to incorporate into his position the biblical teaching on the State and justice which Jerram and I emphasise.

b. God's purposes for human kind

Romans 13 seems to me to be giving *positive* instruction about the State, whose God-given 'authority' and God-given 'ministry' are each affirmed three times.

The contrast in Romans 12.17 and 19 between 'do not repay' and 'I will repay', and between 'do not take revenge' and 'it is mine to avenge' does not teach a double standard of morality, the Christian behaving according to one ethic, the State according to another. The contrast is not primarily between individual and collective (i.e. state) responsibilities, nor between Christian people and secular authorities, but between the responses to evil which are appropriate to *human beings* on the one hand and to *God* on the other. Only God is judge. We may not play judge as individuals. It is God who judges, either through the State or on the last day.

This reality is apparent in the passion of Christ. For even while praying for his persecutors' forgiveness, and refusing to retaliate, 'he entrusted himself (and, it seems, his cause) to him who judges justly' (1 Pet. 2.23). Thus, even when giving himself for our *salvation*, the necessity of divine *judgement* on evil was not absent from his mind. Even when praying for God's *mercy*, he did not forget God's *justice*. Just judgement was God's prerogative, however; it was not his.

c. The legitimacy of extrapolation

To extrapolate the teaching of Romans 12—13 from domestic justice to warfare can be justified only if warfare may be viewed as an act of justice. It is true that the waging of war is a very different activity from the administration of law and order, since in declaring war a State is acting as judge in its own cause (there being as yet no independent, international arbiter); and the set procedures and dispassionate atmosphere of the lawcourt have no parallel on the battlefield. Nevertheless, as Oliver O'Donovan argued in his study, *In Pursuit of a Christian View of War* (Grove booklets, 1977), the development of the just war theory 'represented a systematic attempt to interpret acts of war by analogy with acts of civil government', and so to see them as belonging to 'the context of the administration of justice' and as subject to 'the restraining standards of executive justice'.

d. The context in which killing would be justified

We need to pay proper attention to the biblical horror of blood-shedding, which is due to the fact that human blood symbolises the life of Godlike human beings (Gen. 9.6). It is true that most Old Testament references to the shedding of innocent blood relate to peacetime conditions, but this does not seem to me to affect the principle, namely that the blood of Godlike human beings is sacrosanct and may be shed *only by specific divine warrant*.

What then, about the wholesale slaughters of the Old Testament, which included women and children? Some (e.g. the Flood and the destruction of Sodom) were direct acts of God's judgement and could not therefore be used as models for human imitation. Others (like the extermination of the Canaanites) were *sui generis*, being essential to the history of salvation at that particular moment (by the preservation of the covenant people), and can therefore have no parallel today. 'Just war' there may be, but not 'holy war'. As for the children being punished for their fathers' sins, this fact was never transferred to the lawcourts as a principle to be observed in the administration of justice. On the contrary, in the lawcourts personal guilt had to be established. If therefore it is legitimate to think of a just war as an act of justice, then the solidarity principle does not apply. Instead, every possible step should be taken to preserve the distinction between the innocent and the guilty.

PART TWO

THE BASIS OF THE VIEWS

CROSS-EXAMINED

Chapter Four

NOT ALL APPROACHES TO THE BIBLE ARE EQUALLY VALID

Richard Baukham and Gordon McConville

1. Hermeneutical starting-points

One of the biggest problems in the discussion between the three participants is that they approach the subject in sharply divergent ways. John Stott begins with the authority and ministry of the State, as set out in Romans 12.17—13.7. He sees the State's authority in the punishment of evildoers as the outworking of God's wrath, but limited by the prohibition of shedding innocent blood. Jerram Barrs begins with the idea of God's justice, drawing on a large number of Old Testament texts and tracing the theme into the New Testament, to show that the expression of God's justice in the world is fundamental and continuing. Alan Kreider begins with the teaching of Jesus and particularly the unparalleled and unqualified commandment to love one's enemy.

These starting-points are not arbitrary, but reflect the overall positions of each, and have given the discussion its particular shape. The problem is, however, that already at this stage in each case hermeneutical assumptions have been made. John Stott and Jerram Barrs stress the continuity between the Testaments, while Alan Kreider stresses their discontinuity. Neither approach can be pronounced 'correct' in any simple way. There are dangers inherent in both. Where continuity is stressed and, as a corollary, the Old Testament is effectively made the starting-point, the danger is either of using inappropriate texts or using texts inappropriately. The following examples are intended merely to illustrate this point, not to settle any specific issues.

i. The use made of Leviticus 17.11 and Deuteronomy 12.23 to illustrate the life-blood principle begs the question as to whether what some people call the 'ceremonial' laws may still be relevant for Christians. (One assumes that the position adopted by the Jerusalem Council in Acts 15 is a kind of compromise between the binding force of the law for Jews and freedom in Christ for Gentiles.)

ii. The prophetic condemnations of spilling blood (e.g. Jer. 7.5ff.; 19.4) do not envisage war situations. John Stott responds that the prohibition of shedding blood applies in principle to war situations also (citing Genesis 9.6). But the significance of the Genesis statement itself requires demonstration before it can be used as a general principle to cover a wide variety of situations.

Blood was in fact spilled in divinely-sanctioned wars (as in judicial executions). However, the problem in appealing to Genesis 9.6 as a principle which limits bloodshed in war is that the Bible does not appear to use it anywhere in this way.

Prohibition of the killing of the innocent, therefore, is difficult to apply directly to proposals for limiting warfare, because the question raised by war is precisely when the prohibition does not apply.

Furthermore, if a war is claimed to be 'just', the claim must be made on other grounds than those which justify ancient Israel's participation in wars (see the next section). Such grounds, if they can be found, require a theory of war which can cope with ideas such as 'innocence'. In other words, the biblical injunction against the shedding of blood, even granted its universality in principle, cannot be applied 'neat' without begging questions inherent in the concrete situation to which it is applied.

iii. In general Jerram Barrs' citing of Old Testament texts lacks a theory of how God's expression of his will and character in the context of his relationship with Israel becomes relevant for the conduct of nations today. Some of the texts cited are not specifically pertinent even to the political responsibilities of Israel (e.g. Ps. 146.7–9; Prov. 17.15). Those which are still beg the question how texts, whose meaning is clear when the people of God are coextensive with a political entity, can become meaningful when the people of God is no longer such an entity (e.g. Josh. 6.21; Ps. 144.1).

iv. A final point may be made on the choice of texts. Jerram Barrs has focused largely on the State's responsibility to reflect God's character as judge. He is aware that this implies the defence of the poor. Yet the State as 'judge' is perhaps a little one-sided. The work of government is also sometimes seen as having a dimension of spirit-filled creativity (e.g. Joseph in Egypt). In using the Old Testament for a Christian view of government, texts should be chosen to show the positive possibilities for human government under God.

On the other hand, where discontinuity between the Testaments is stressed problems of a different sort arise. Alan Kreider has indeed provided a rationale for his position by claiming that Jesus' statements about love are definitive concerning the Christian's abstention from all war.

It is arguable that the reliability of this particular rationale must turn on the exegesis of those particular texts which deal with love of the enemy. (They are disputed by Christians.) Yet exegesis of given texts cannot ultimately be done in isolation from an understanding of biblical theology as a whole. Alan Kreider would strengthen his case by providing a counter-proposal to the argument that Israel, in her political structures, manifests something fundamental and universal about the created order in which all human beings are necessarily involved. He would strengthen it further if he could show that Romans 13 is in principle less about the participation of God's people in government than are the Books of Daniel or Esther. In both these latter cases free participation in government is combined with a loyalty to God which produces conflict with the State. This conflict, however, is never over the question of the State's right to 'bear the sword'.

2. Old Testament wars

Old Testament wars are an important component of Jerram Barrs' original argument, although, since his thinking in this area is on the move, he may not wish now to stand by everything he first stated. In his original argument Old Testament wars seem to contribute significantly to his concept of what a just war is. John Stott's rather different concept of a just war is not based on Old Testament wars. It springs from an extrapolation of the State's authority as laid down in Romans 13 and limited by general, biblical moral principles, as these have been applied over the centuries in the just war tradition.

All seem agreed that to some extent at least the wars of Old Testament Israel were *sui generis*, and so, like many other aspects of the law, they cannot be used as straightforward blueprints for modern practice. However, we still need to ask to *what* extent are they *sui generis*, and is it possible to discern underlying principles which are still valid today?

Any attempt to discern such principles must engage in a serious theological and historical-contextual study of Old Testament ideas on war. It should take account of the following main considerations:

i. All of Israel's wars were 'holy' wars (Deut. 20.1–4), i.e. wars in which God fought with and on behalf of his people against his and their enemies. As the wars of God's own people, they had a special role in God's salvation-historical purpose which no other wars can have. God's New Testament people, the Church, have no wars of their own (even if they may participate in the wars of a secular state).

The New Testament applies 'holy war' language to the Church, but reinterprets it in terms of spiritual warfare, suffering witness and church discipline.

Israel's wars *as holy wars* are comparable to the temple, the priesthood, the rules regarding uncleanness and other features of the Old Testament people of God which the new covenant in Christ makes obsolete, in the sense that for the Church other things replace them.

Two major consequences follow from the new reality of Jesus Christ. Firstly, the Church may not fight crusades. Secondly, no State may consider itself God's people, fighting his wars against his enemies.

It is important therefore to see that principles derived from Israel's wars will be applicable to modern wars *only if* they can be convincingly distinguished and detached from the specifically 'holy war' features of all Israel's wars.

ii. Deuteronomy 20 makes a clear distinction between two types of ('holy') war: against the inhabitants of the promised land   (Deut. 20.16–18)   and   against   other   nations (Deut. 20.10–15). These two types of war are distinguished in aim and method: the first aims at the massacre of 'all who breathe', while the second aims at victory, which may be achieved without bloodshed (Deut. 20.11) and should not require total slaughter (Deut. 20.13–14).

The first of these two types of war has features which seem to have coloured Jerram Barrs' understanding of a just war: the war is understood as a form of death penalty, the killing is indiscriminate (whole populations are massacred), and the general wickedness of the enemy (not simply their aggression against Israel) helps to justify the war. However, if these are taken to be basic principles of this particular type of war, it must be recognised that they are inapplicable to any other type. They are strictly unique features of this one category of Old Testament holy war.

This can be seen, if it is asked in what terms the war against the Canaanites, having these features, was considered just. Its justice depended on three factors:

(a) The practice of the ban. This practice, which Israel shared with her neighbours, became in Israel a form of judicial sentence executed on God's behalf (it also applied to Israelite cities guilty of idolatry, Deut. 13.12–18). Thus the aim of these wars was the judicial execution of guilty people (especially idolaters).

(b) The evil of those placed under the ban was a temptation to God's people (Deut. 20.18). The execution was not merely retributive, but aimed at removing a criminal influence. Thus Israel did not have a general commission to massacre all wicked nations, but only those which were a moral danger to herself.

(c) God had given Israel the land. Otherwise, the conquest would not be justified, and the grave moral temptation would not be relevant.

It should be evident that these three factors are necessarily unique to Israel in her special relationship to God and in her special place in salvation history.

iii. The possibility of finding underlying principles which are still valid is more open in the case of the second type of Old Testament holy war, as regulated in Deuteronomy 20.10–15. This type of war is not aimed at genocide, but simply at victory, if possible without bloodshed (Deut. 20.11).

However, it is not at all easy to discern underlying principles within this passage as it stands. The extraction of principles valid for all time and in all situations is even more difficult since these would have to be distinguished *both* from 'holy war' principles applicable only to Old Testament Israel *and* from features which could be seen as 'accommodation' to the practice of war in ancient Israel's environment. To discern the latter requires study of the practice of war not only in the Old Testament but also in the ancient Near East.

iv. The question of 'accommodation' could rightly be pursued by using the analogy of slavery in Old Testament Israel. The Old Testament laws on slavery are to be regarded as concessive and regulatory. They merely tolerated an institution which Israel shared with the rest of the ancient world and humanised it as far as possible. We do not now consider that they should have been an impediment to the abolition of slavery, which follows from fundamental biblical principles and even from the *tendency* of the slavery laws themselves.

Similarly, the Old Testament legislation on war is no impediment either to the much greater humanisation of the practice of war or even to the abolition of war, if fundamental biblical principles lead us to work for these. The legitimacy of Old Testament Israel's wars need not mean that there must always be wars, still less that wars must always be fought with no more restraint or mercy than was required of Israel. Arguments about 'realism' here (that Old Testament laws are realistic in view of the constant facts of the sinful human condition) should be viewed with great caution, seeing that they were also used historically against the abolition of slavery.

v. Finally, the question whether Old Testament wars rest on basic principles which should still legitimise and regulate war must be considered in relation to the general hermeneutical question of the relationship between the teaching of Jesus and the continued validity of Old Testament legal principles. The participants are by no means agreed on this vital issue.

That Jesus' teaching should affect our understanding of the issues being debated seems to follow from two important considerations:

(a) Jesus' purpose in interpreting the law was precisely to identify its fundamental principles and (as in the case of divorce) to extend these principles in cases where the Old Testament law represented an accommodation.

(b) Jesus identified love as the all-encompassing principle of the law (Matt. 22.40), and extended the principle of love of neighbour, which in the Old Testament law itself referred only to fellow-Israelites (Lev. 19.18), to include national enemies (Matt. 5.43–54; Luke 10.29–37).

This line of approach suggests that areas of Old Testament legislation concerned with Israel's relation to her national enemies are precisely (some of) the areas in which Jesus is demanding a more consistent application of the law's own principle of love. When Israel went to war, the law did not require her actions to be motivated by love for her enemies; Jesus, however, does require this.

Having stressed these points, it also has to be acknowledged that in this whole area of the relationship between law and love there is still substantial disagreement in interpretation. For example, the idea that Jesus made love the principle of *all* law is contested and may not be capable of supplying an adequate basis for making and enforcing laws designed to restrain and punish evildoers.

3. *Love and justice*

On the general question of the relationship of love and justice – so often a source of confusion in Christian discussion of this kind of issue – the participants seem agreed. Justice and love are not to be opposed, but are in harmony in the nature of God and ideally also in human activity. Justice is an expression of love, which must at least perform what justice requires, though it may also go beyond justice. Even the State must go beyond a narrow concept of retributive justice, in showing mercy, implementing forgiveness, aiming at reformatory punishment and engaging in active concern for the needy and the oppressed.

At the same time, love can never be expressed at the expense of justice, since the community's good can never be secured by injustice. It may be that in certain circumstances the demands of love and justice will have to be in conflict.

It is far too simplistic, therefore, to consider that pacifists base their arguments on love and non-pacifists on justice. Jerram Barrs, for example, stresses that it is the love of one's neighbour which justifies wars of intervention on behalf of the oppressed. Alan Kreider argues that wars often, if not always, increase injustice rather than justice.

There is, therefore, a substantially agreed framework within which to discuss the problem of the just and loving nature of war. The questions, however, remain. Exactly how do we determine the content of justice in biblical terms? Can there be situations in which love for most people or for oppressed people requires that some people be killed? Or, as Alan Kreider holds, must the Christian duty to love everyone (particularly the oppressor) rule out the killing of anyone? Is killing the ultimate demonstration that love is absent, so that it must be wholly ruled out for Christians (Alan Kreider), or can it sometimes be an expression of love (Jerram Barrs, John Stott)? In the nuclear situation what *limits* does love set on the legitimate aims and means of war? All these questions require fuller study.

4. *Domestic and international justice*

Though the key passage of Romans 13 has been the object of considerable debate, it seems the participants are now agreed that it does describe government as a good activity. It can therefore be a proper sphere of Christian service, even though Paul is not here actually envisaging Christians in government. Alan Kreider still has difficulty at this point, for if the 'sword' involves the exercise of capital punishment, then in his view this would be inconsistent with the Christian vocation.

However, the real issue in the debate about war is whether (given that Paul is only talking about domestic justice) the government's right to wage wars can be deduced from this passage by arguing that it is a legitimate extension of the government's responsibility for domestic justice.

The analogy between law-enforcement at home and just wars has the status of a hermeneutical key for Jerram Barrs and John Stott. For the former the analogy implies implicitly that killing in war is comparable to the death penalty at home.

It is now agreed by all that the Bible does not make this analogy explicitly. John Stott indicated in his hermeneutical statement that Romans 13 could only apply to international justice by extrapolation. He believed that such extrapolation was possible, provided that warfare may be viewed as an act of justice. He is thus within the traditional just war theory, which represents an attempt to limit warfare by bringing it within the realm of the administration of justice: a war to be justified should be capable of being pronounced just by one who was legally competent to do so.

There are, of course, important differences between justice

exercised at home and justice as it may be achieved through war. John Stott accepts that the analogy is not exact. In domestic courts of law the State arbitrates independently between the parties. In war the State is itself one of the parties. This means that the way in which the State administers justice in war – if it can do so – differs from the way in which it does so at home at least in respect of the element of independent arbitration. It differs also in respect of execution. In war – even a 'just' war – it is not necessarily the guilty who die. Or at least the idea of guilt, if appropriate at all, must be very different from that which operates in a lawcourt. The conduct of war, even when it is discriminate (i.e. directed only towards the armed forces of another State), still results in the death of individuals who have committed no crime.

These are weighty considerations. The argument for the analogy between the implementation of domestic and international justice may still be acceptable if the following considerations hold:

i. A nation's armed forces representatively bear the guilt (somehow established) of the nation. However, to justify civilian casualities, it would be necessary to establish that all members of the nation corporately share in the guilt of those in authority.

ii. Some process, which takes the place of the independent arbitration of the lawcourt, has the moral and legal authority to declare that a nation at war is acting justly.

The possibility of this kind of arbitration is the central objective of traditional just war theory, as opposed to an ideal of collective self-defence. One way of achieving it might be if a number of nations agree together that war should be waged. However, shared self-interest is likely to mean that objectivity has not been attained.

Ideally an essentially diverse body like the UN seems best fitted, in terms of moral theory, to meet the main requirement of not having a particular vested interest in the legal and ethical decision. Such a body, however, is certainly the least suitable in terms of the practical possibility of actually reaching a judicious judgement. The International Court at the Hague, made up of experts in international law, is probably the least questionable institution available for deciding objectively on the merits of the case.

Alternatively it may be argued that the State is in principle itself capable of making the sort of moral decision that involves going to war. Here it should be borne in mind that classical just war thinking insisted that the defence of the innocent, must figure prominently in the motivation for going to war (rather than self-defence.)

At this point we are close to the argument concerning love and justice where we noted that Jerram Barrs stressed that the love of neighbour can justify wars of intervention on behalf of the oppressed. If the State is capable of love then it may have the necessary moral qualification to make war. The example of the international response to the crisis of starvation in Ethiopia (1984–6) shows that the boundary between the individual, interest groups and the State in the expression of love is not necessarily cut and dried.

5. Solidarity

The idea of national solidarity seems to have been used rather opportunistically instead of being carefully examined in its Old Testament context to see whether it can legitimately be applied at all to the modern conduct of war.

There are some passages in the Old Testament which seem to recognise a kind of solidarity under divine judgement, which may include solidarity across several generations (Exod. 20.5). In some instances this principle apparently affects humanly executed judgements (Deut. 23.3–6; 25.17–19; Josh. 7.24; 1 Sam. 15.2–3; 2 Sam. 21.1–14). But if we take those as models, we should be clear what they involve: punishing the children with the parents or punishing a whole nation for the sins of its ancestors. Moreover, the law specifically forbade the use of this principle in the ordinary administration of justice (Deut. 24.16).

The story of Sodom and Gomorrah, including Abraham's intercession and the rescue of Lot and his daughters, is not so much an illustration of the principle as a protest against it (Gen. 18.25: 'Far be it from you to do such a thing – to kill the righteous with the wicked. . . . Will not the judge of all the earth do right?'). Similarly Ezekiel 18 appears to be a thoroughgoing rejection of solidarity as a principle of divine justice.

There are surely real tensions here in Old Testament teaching, which cannot be adequately appropriated for the purposes of the debate about war by a 'flat' hermeneutic which puts all these passages on the same level and simply tries to harmonise them. Above all, we must not, when convenient to do so, exploit some of the passages to justify some of our actions and others to justify other actions.

6. *Understanding the contemporary issue*

The dangers of the present international situation have clearly been the context of the debate. Each participant recognises that there can be no proper hermeneutic that does not deal with the application of principles to the world as it is.

There are, however, two novel features of the nuclear situation, which alongside an indication of the problems for interpretation which have arisen in the debate, are particularly worth noting:

i. Nuclear weapons are, in one degree or another, indiscriminate: not only do they kill large numbers of civilians immediately but also they do such damage to the environment that life is jeopardised or made impossible for countless others, including millions living in nations not at war and further millions not yet born. The fact that, if used, nuclear weapons would threaten the very existence and continuity of creation itself should make any responsible human agency pause and tremble.

ii. The doctrine of nuclear deterrence has, as John Stott recognises, built-in logical and moral difficulties. Jerram Barrs takes the view that it is justifiable to *threaten* use of nuclear weapons in order to achieve the real end, namely that none should be used. John Stott's position is slightly different, namely that it is justifiable to *possess* nuclear weapons without the intention to use them. This is open to the acknowledged objection, on strategic grounds, that possession is meaningless unless there is every intention to use the weapons as a last resort, and on moral grounds that a threat without the intention to carry it out is a deceitful act.

Furthermore, except in the case of a pre-emptive strike (widely held to be morally less acceptable than a declared intention only to use nuclear weapons as a response to an overwhelming act of aggression), the use of nuclear weapons could only be retaliatory. If such a situation arose, deterrence would, by definition, have failed in its stated aim. The launch of nuclear warheads in that situation would have no more significance than useless revenge.

These underlying problems present considerable, though recognised, difficulties for the positions taken by Jerram Barrs and John Stott. Nevertheless, it needs to be said that the realities of the situation are changing fast. One element in the change is the increasing sophistication (and therefore discrimination) of nuclear weapons. John Stott notes, rightly, there is yet little comfort to draw from these developments.

It is important that Christians have views which they express publicly, not only on the underlying issues, but on the ever-changing options which are the stuff of current controversy in the corridors of power. One can only hope that among some of those options there are lesser evils than any of those we are forced to choose at the moment.

Chapter Five

WITNESSES FOR THE

DEFENCE

Jerram Barrs

1. A hermeneutical starting-point

I want to re-affirm my conviction that all biblical teaching about specific issues and consequently all our moral understanding needs to be related to basic biblical themes, in particular to the doctrines of God, creation, fall and man as God's image-bearer.

Whether we are discussing the moral requirements for individuals, the calling of governments or the way nations are to relate to each other in peacetime or in war, we need to bring everything back to the touchstone of God's own character. Scripture makes it clear that all human behaviour, whether at the personal or national level, is to be judged against God's revelation of his own justice, holiness, mercy and love. This is clearly true both in the Old Testament and the New (Lev. 19; Matt. 5.43–8; 1 Pet. 1.15, 16; Eph. 4.32—5:2; 1 John 4.7–21). God's commandment to man and woman to rule the earth is a clear application of this call to be like God for he is the ruler of all (Gen. 1.28). Indeed, all rule by human persons partakes of this godlikeness, and that is why the rulers of all nations (and not just Israel) are termed 'gods' in Psalm 82 and John 10.34–5, and it is also why governing authorities are declared to be established by God in Romans 13.1. It is because of this that we are to submit to them for the Lord's sake and because of conscience (1 Pet. 2.13; Rom. 13.5).

Our hermeneutical assessors suggest that with this starting point I might have a 'flat' approach to Scripture. I can only agree with this assessment in so far as they may mean that regarding God's character as unchanging is a 'flat' interpretation. My view allows me to see the various stages in the history of redemption in their differences and yet insist that there is a fundamental unity which underlies the differences.

For example, Israel has a unique calling in history to be the people of God occupying a particular geographical situation for a set period of time. As such they were to be a light to the nations around and the place of preparation for the coming of Christ. The laws that they were given and the institutions of government established among them by God reflect both this temporary calling and fundamental principles derived from God's character.

As an illustration, consider the death penalty for false prophecy, idolatry, adultery, homosexuality and perjury in capital cases. There is in this penalty not the display of a primitive and unlettered understanding of God, later set aside by Christ, but rather a dramatic account of what God considers to be of basic importance to the well-being of individual human life and the life of nations. In the New Testament the particular aspect of Israel as God's nation is set aside. The death penalty is replaced by church discipline for each of these sins. Yet, that does not mean that we are to consider false teaching, adultery or homosexuality as less serious. Some of the hardest words spoken by Jesus are about false teaching. The eternal penalty will be far more severe than the death penalty (Luke 17.1–2). Equally, Paul makes powerful denunciations of sexual sin and slander (1 Cor. 6.9–10). He has learnt from the severity of the Old Testament penalties, as we must too, that whether we are considering our own individual holiness, church discipline, or areas where we need to press for change in the values and laws of our societies that these activities are dangerously wrong. Not that we should campaign for the death penalty for these sins, but rather, that these matters become priorities for us and for society – for they are important to God.

Similarly, in the Sermon on the Mount, Jesus is not giving us a new set of ethical precepts. Rather, he is calling us back to the original principles which lie behind the Law of Moses, which are embodied in it, and which are distorted or ignored by the Pharisees in their search for a legalistic righteousness in which they could take pride. That is clearly the context of the Sermon on the Mount (Matt. 5.17–20). Even love for enemies is present in the Mosiac law (Exod. 23.4–5; Deut. 22.1–4), as is the command to love aliens in the same way as a brother Israelite (Exod. 22.21; Lev. 24.22; Ps. 146.9).

I agree with Alan Kreider that Jesus' teaching in the Sermon on the Mount is like a key. However, the key Jesus gives us there is how to understand the Old Testament law: that is, that we are to look for the enduring principles that underlie it and predate it – principles which come from the character of God.

Therefore, we can take any statement about government authority or about the waging of war, even holy war, and look for the principles that are taught in it.

2. Domestic and international justice

This subject is closely related to the wider hermeneutical issue and I see no reason why one cannot regard principles valid in the enforcement of law at home as applicable to relationships between nations.

Indeed, on reflection, I suggest that there is an explicit analogy between the death penalty at home and killing in war. The first biblical prohibition against murder comes in Genesis 9.6–7. There it is stated as a general principle that, if one man kills another man, his life is forfeit. The context is not one of the State using the sword, but rather a general prohibition and penalty applicable to the human race in all circumstances – the reason given being the unique dignity of man as the image of God. In later revelation we see this applied to the 'avenger of blood', to the State's use of sword, and to warfare. For what is an aggressive war but the murdering and plundering of innocent people? The only recourse in the case of the murder of innocent people in warfare is to take up the instruments of war oneself. There will, of course, be no judicial body to appeal to in the nature of the case. Perhaps it is akin to the 'avenger of blood' in Israel whose responsibility was to pursue the murderer. In the nation of Israel the elders of the community had to decide whether the case was manslaughter or murder. In the case of warfare the nation has to decide for itself whether the war is just or unjust. This creates difficulties; nevertheless, there is no real alternative.

In the first chapter of Amos there are several clear examples of the way God requires the actions of nations – including their waging of war – to be judged in the same way as the behaviour of individuals. Pagan nations which did not have the direct revelation of God in Scripture but only the law written on their consciences are pronounced guilty by God. Their crimes were murder, barbarous slave trading, breaking treaties of brotherhood, stifling compassion, atrocities against the weak, abuse of dead bodies, and again widespread and appalling murder. The penalty pronounced against them was defeat and death in war. There are many examples like this throughout the prophets where God judges atrocities committed in waging war by defeat in war. The crimes listed are those which deserve the severest penalties within a nation, and so they receive the same penalty between nations.

States are judged like individuals because they are made up of individuals, and it is human persons accountable to God who make the decisions of nations. Therefore it is appropriate to speak of love, compassion, brotherhood, the defence of the oppressed, sin, murder, restraint of evil and punishment for crime when we are speaking about nations, just as much as when we speak about individuals. We find this throughout God's Word. To deny that there is a direct analogy between domestic and international justice and mercy implies ignoring large sections of God's Word which uses a common language for both, flying in the face of common sense, and leaving the most powerful forces of evil in the world unrestrained, undeterred and unpunished. It would also leave the most needy people in the world largely unhelped and with no hope of rescue. That is hardly fulfilling our mandate to rule under God as his image-bearers.

3. Contemporary issues

I recognise that there are particular moral difficulties raised by nuclear deterrence and by the possibility of nuclear war: the destructive power of the weapons, the fear of escalation leading to a holocaust, and the questionable morality of deterrence based on threatening destruction. Some of these I have tried to answer in Chapter 1, though I do not feel entirely comfortable with my answers. This is only partly because of the nuclear issue, for discussion of war, killing, deterrence and the world situation is never comforting because these are arenas where the sinfulness of the human race is most dramatically displayed.

There are, in addition, some particular questions we face at the present time. Can the West be trusted when it has a nuclear first strike policy? Does not this commitment to reply to a Warsaw Pact conventional attack with a NATO nuclear response undermine the protestations of peaceful intention by Western governments? To answer this question we must understand what has happened since 1945. After World War II Western European governments invited the United States to defend their countries because of fear of the advance of the Soviet army across Europe at the end of the war. NATO developed its deterrent policy of nuclear arsenals as an attempt to deal with this threat. Coming up to our own time NATO is dependent on nuclear weapons both to deter a nuclear attack by the Warsaw Pact and also to deter a conventional attack by the Warsaw Pact. Why is this? There are two reasons, the first being that the Warsaw Pact has huge conventional forces in Eastern Europe. The second reason is that the United States nuclear umbrella has been a cheap way for Western European governments to provide deterrence against the superior Soviet conventional forces. It was felt that Western European populations would not tolerate the expense of providing adequate conventional weapons systems or adequate standing armies.

We now find ourselves in the strange situation where many Western Europeans feel they need protection from the United States as much as or even more than from the Soviet Union. Talk by some American generals about a European theatre of limited nuclear war understandably fills people with fear. President Reagan speaking of the Soviet Union as 'an evil empire' increases people's sense of insecurity and foreboding even if they know in their hearts that it is an accurate statement. There is in Western Europe a desperate need for reassurance about the future, and every accident to a nuclear submarine or at a nuclear plant increases this need. This is particularly so after Chernobyl made everyone aware of the consequences of even a limited nuclear exchange. What is to be done about this?

First it seems essential that Western Europe and other nations must take more responsibility for their own defence. It is no accident that those European nations which have relied least on the American nuclear umbrella are those with the smallest peace movements. Switzerland, Sweden and France have all been much more determined to develop adequate forces and weapons themselves. Switzerland and Sweden may be technically neutral but that does not mean they are naïve or romantic about the fact that history proves the necessity of always being well armed and well prepared if war is to be avoided and deterred. The rest of Western Europe, and in particular the NATO countries, need to learn from this fact and be prepared both to increase their armed forces and to spend more on conventional weapons.

Second it seems that NATO's policy of relying on nuclear weapons to deter both nuclear and conventional attack is inherently unstable. Such a policy runs the risk of its bluff being called and the Soviet Union assuming that, especially after Chernobyl, no NATO government would in reality carry out its first strike commitment for fear of escalation. This factor underlies the urgent need for NATO to make sure it has more adequate conventional forces.

Third we must be realistic enough to recognise that there are radical differences between the Soviet Union and Western governments. The West, including the USA, is full of injustices and problems: the killing of the unborn, racial discrimination, family breakdown, massive unemployment, sexual immorality, inner city decay. These need urgent attention and the Christian, being both light and salt, must be the first to show a different example and work for improvements. Yet by recognising that there is an objective standard against which crime and evil behaviour can be measured and found wanting we also acknowledge that there is still a rule of law. In addition, there is value placed on the life of each person which prevents people being regarded as pawns to be sacrificed for the good of the State. Also, there is a recognition in our structures of government and law that those in power are sinful and that therefore there are checks and balances which restrain the power given to any individual or government. Our leaders are accountable to their people and may be removed from office, either by election or by judicial process if they themselves break the law.

We must admit that each of these strengths in Western society is being undermined at present. This should cause the Christian great sorrow, leading us to repentance and a determined effort to fight for their survival, for all of these strengths have their roots in a biblical view of man and the world and exist because of the efforts of Christians and those influenced by a Christian world view who have struggled to affect society and its institutions in these directions. Partly owing to the Church's neglect and retreat from involvement in the nation these gains are in danger of dissolution. Yet they still remain and give us the freedoms we continue to enjoy.

The Soviet Union, on the other hand, has none of these strengths. Marxism as a philosophy, and the Russian government in practice, both refuse to recognise the rule of law. There are no objective standards of right and wrong in Soviet society, but simply government decrees about what is seen to be useful for the State. There is no value placed on the life of the individual; thus people can be destroyed or put in labour camps, prisons or psychiatric institutions simply because of their beliefs. There is no recognition in the structures of government and law that rulers are sinful and so there are very few restraints on the power of Soviet leaders. The only restraint comes from the struggle for power and privilege amongst those whom the party machine has created into the largest, most privileged aristocracy in the history of the human race. Finally, the leaders are not accountable to their people, for there are no elections which allow a meaningful democratic choice, nor can the leaders be restrained by the courts. The courts are simply the instruments of the rulers' abuse of power.

This totalitarian nature of Soviet government has made the people in the USSR some of the most oppressed in history. It means too that many other nations are kept in unwilling bondage as part of the Soviet Empire so that walls and fences have to be built to keep the citizens at home.

The Christian must be realistic and recognise that a radical difference exists between these two systems of government. In addition, wishful thinking whenever a new Soviet leader appears is no substitute for adequate defence and hard bargaining at the negotiating table. While Mr Gorbachev certainly seems to be attempting to change the economic system in the Soviet Union (as China has very successfully been doing), there is little evidence as yet that he has any desire to lessen the rigid control of government and the party over every other aspect of the people's daily lives.

This realism about the differences of government and social structure and consequent uncertainty about Soviet intentions should not lead to abandoning discussions and interaction between the superpowers. Realism is a much better basis than *naïveté* for negotiation and for arms reduction talks. Our governments must be pressed to work, from a realistic basis, for ways to bring mutual, verifiable disarmament, for it seems absurd that such enormous stockpiles of nuclear weapons should be necessary to maintain a credible deterrent and to prevent the outbreak of war.

Meanwhile what is needed is not panic, not a failure of nerve, and not the cry for 'peace' when there is no peace. Rather we need to have confidence in the Lord and in a biblical view of history. We need to work for justice and mercy at home, beginning with our own lives and gradually pervading society as a whole. We need to maintain an adequate nuclear deterrent, while working for nuclear arms reduction. We need to pay more attention to conventional defence and our own European responsibility. We need to pray for the people in the Soviet Union and its satellites, to pray that they might have the freedom to hear God's word, and that the system which oppresses them might be replaced by one concerned for justice and peace. We need to believe that no human power will last for ever and that God is the ruler of all nations and kingdoms. And we need to say 'Come, Lord Jesus, come and reign and bring perfect peace and justice to this earth.'

Alan Kreider

4. *The challenge to faithful involvement*

It has been a privilege and a pleasure to take part in the conversations which this book records. The interchange, in many settings, between Jerram Barrs, John Stott and myself have challenged me as a Christian and as a Bible-reader. I am also grateful to Richard Bauckham and Gordon McConville for the careful way they have listened to us and read our materials, and for the penetrating comments that they make in their hermeneutical assessment.

In all the interchanges I have sensed a recurrent challenge to me that I am advocating withdrawal from the world; that my understanding of the Bible leads me to retreat from the created order, in which human beings are necessarily involved. I take this challenge seriously, for I come from the Anabaptist-Mennonite tradition which, although its history is varied, has often been tempted (or pushed) to withdraw from the central insitutions of 'worldly' society to create Christian counter-cultures. Often this was a response to persecution by other Christians, Catholic and Protestant alike. As I seek to be a disciple of Jesus today, I must struggle with this heritage of 'separation'. At the same time, I must respond to the prejudices of Christians who, representing the dominant traditions of Western Christendom, have forced my tradition to withdraw and then reproach us as sectarian withdrawers, of having nothing to say to the real world.

The challenge, then, cuts both ways and gives us a common task. The task, as Jesus puts it, is to be 'the salt of the earth' (Matt. 5.13), both scattered in the world and yet distinct from it. As I have listened to Jesus stating this vision, I have been challenged to allow him to scatter me and members of my tradition into all parts, in order to demonstrate our concern for the world that God loves and to find ways of being more involved in it for the sake of his kingdom. My tradition needs, for example, not just to denounce the arms race, but to find new ways of participating in God's world-wide work of peace-making. Whenever I speak and counsel people today, I urge them not to withdraw from the world. But I also urge them to hunt for ways of taking part in it that are salty: distinctive and Jesus-like. This may be a part of the task which challenges other Christian traditions. In the world today we are confronted with problems of unprecedented gravity. One of these has to do with people and missiles. It is often called militarism. Do Christians who are involved in military matters have anything specifically, distinctively Christian to say about the assumptions which undergird their profession? As I struggle to repent of unfaithfulness and become more involved, I would humbly ask those whose traditions have always stressed active partici-pation: do you at times echo the world's thoughts? Jesus' call beckons us all, whatever historical tradition we may come from.

5. Dealing with the points raised

First, the *hermeneutical starting-point*. The assessors have asserted that I stress 'the discontinuity between the Testaments', but do I? It is true that I start with Jesus Christ. I am genuinely puzzled why other Christians do not. We confess that he and the Father are one, that he is God's perfect and final revelation of himself. I find it appropriate, therefore, in our ethics, to start with him to observe how he taught and behaved, and to see how he authoritatively dealt with the Old Testament. At times, our assessors have observed, Jesus found the Old Testament law to be provisional, 'concessive and regulative', as they put it (as in Matt. 19.8). Jesus, I am convinced should be our hermeneutical key as we read the Old Testament. Similarly in the New Testament we observe Jesus forming a movement of men and women who, filled by the Holy Spirit, applied his teachings and lifestyle to the congregations which they founded, and who, in all their behaviour, were determined to 'walk in the way in which he walked' (1 John 2.6).

If this is so, perhaps we should read Paul and Peter through the Gospel accounts of Jesus, for they were, after all, disciples of the Master, rather than vice-versa. So, Jesus should be our hermeneutical key to the New Testament as well as the Old. With the principle of *Jesus as the hermeneutical key*, certain questions will be less difficult. For example, why do we not permit polygamy or stone people for adultery? I have deep trouble with any approach that sees Jesus Christ as normative for the way we are saved but which makes little or no difference to the way 'saved' people live. As Christians we are, unapologetically, Jesus people.

However, by starting with Jesus, I do not mean to stress a discontinuity between the Testaments. Indeed, the more I have learned about Jesus, the more I have realised how much his person, and his statement of the good news, are products of the Old Testament, indeed are fulfilments of its longing for a deeper expression of salvation in a new era of salvation history (e.g. Jer. 31.31–4). Jesus, it seems to me, is the fulfilment of the Old Testament's promises. And the nature of that fulfilment is normative for those who would follow him, whether in the first century or today. Let me cite one example. Jesus lived in an era when many Jewish people used the Old Testament discriminately, opting for the holy war and yet rejecting jubilee economics. But Jesus' fulfilment of the Old Testament was precisely the opposite to that which his contemporaries found congenial. Arguably, the world is in the mess that it's in, because Christians have learned from them rather than from him.

Second, the *mandate for participation*, derived from biblical revelation as a whole. To begin with, the assessors assert that

Israel's political structures manifest 'something fundamental about the created order'. But this statement as it stands needs clarifying. Do these political structures manifest the created order, or one that is fallen? Are the assessors referring to Israel's actual political structures or to normative ones? For example, are they referring to structures created by David and Solomon or to the prescriptions about kingship in Deuteronomy 17.14–17, which forbade the king to engage in the multi-plication of horses (weaponry), wives (alliances, religious syncretism) and silver and gold (massive disparity in wealth)? When we take normative Old Testament politics seriously, they begin to look quite a bit more like the politics of Jesus than the politics of Judah.

The assessors argue further that, in the light of the political activities of Daniel and Esther, Romans 13 implies a mandate for political participation. However, that is not what the text says: it is a mandate for subordination, not participation. Only by a process of analogy and extrapolation can we understand that Romans 13 suggests participation.

I favour political participation by Christians. However, if this participation is faithful to God and his Messiah it won't be easy. The examples which the assessors cite make this abun-dantly clear. For reasons of lifestyle (Dan. 1.8), as well as loyalty to God (the two are not unrelated), these and other participants one could name ended up in hot situations like fiery furnaces. They did not, admittedly, get into trouble because they objected to the State's right to bear the sword. But then these were Old Testament believers. They had not heard Jesus call them into the kingdom in which (to quote the assessors) he would demand 'a more consistent application of the Law's own principle of love'. Participation, therefore, is good, but not at any price. Jesus' disciple Paul understood this well. So, in Romans 12.17 he specifically forbade believers from doing what Romans 13.4 says the State will do: engage in vengeance.

Third, the question of *contentious exegesis*. I cannot accept the assumption that there is a way of reading crucial texts which is not contentious.

For fifteen centuries or so, among the dominant Christian traditions, there has been something approaching a consensus on the meaning of crucial texts such as Matthew 5.43–8 or Romans 13.1–7. These, along with other passages, have been used to make Jesus apolitical, and thus, in effect, to keep the mighty in their seats and send the poor and powerless empty away. Those who disagreed could be marginalised and often persecuted as 'heretics', even though those heretics were intuitively carrying on the way that the pre-Constantinian Christians had read these texts. But today this enforced consensus has broken down. Christianity is no longer socially dominant in the West; indeed, it is no longer primarily Western. The world is now in a situation of crisis in certain areas, particularly those of war and wealth, about which Christians, because there is no longer any general agreement among them, can say nothing distinctive.

Today Christians around the world are re-reading the Bible. They are finding that its good news for the real world means that the long-standing, agreed reading of the crucial texts may have been wrong; indeed, that it may have been death-dealing to our civilisation. These fresh discoveries have a number of causes. I have already alluded to two of these: a profound observation of the real world and new forms of church life which are appropriate to a pilgrim, missionary people in the midst of a non-Christian world. I would also like to point to two others.

One of these is the contribution of scholarship. Expositors have always known that their interpretations must be based on sound exegesis, i.e. that their message to people today must be a product of their struggle with what the texts meant to their writers and first readers/hearers. We often avoid this discipline, citing passages as if they were written directly to use in the 1980s, rather than to men, women and children of the first century. To counteract this mistaken tendency we need to take seriously the painstaking work of scholars, especially those who have, in recent years, uncovered important things about the socio-political setting of the biblical texts. These insights often call into question traditional interpretations. As a result, today there is little consensus. The reading of many biblical texts, therefore, is bound to be contentious. As the Holy Spirit guides us, we must choose the interpretations which best fit the evidence.

The socio-political situation of the interpreter is another major reason why there is no longer an agreed interpretation of certain important texts. Only when the situation of the reader is similar to that of the writer can the task of relating exposition to exegesis become less problematical. A friend of mine, who is a specialist in ethics, once told me that it was only after Constantine came that Christians could really understand what Paul meant in Romans 13. On the contrary, after Constantine it became especially difficult for Christians to understand what Paul was getting at, for they now wielded power in the world. Whereas, weak, marginal and persecuted people find it much easier, for their place in the world is much closer to that which Paul and the Christians in Rome occupied. Each one of us, then, as we read the Bible, must ask not only 'What does the Bible say?', but 'Who are we, as we read the Bible?' Are we in a position to hear God's Word? What do we need to take into account in order to be more open and honest with the text? The assessors, I feel, have not given sufficient weight to this dimension of interpretation, implicit in my hermeneutical statement.

6. *The journey towards fresh understanding and obedience*

Finally, an eirenic point upon which I hope we could all agree. As Evangelicals we confess together that the 'word of God is living and active, sharper than any two-edged sword', and that it invariably pierces to the heart of any matter (Heb. 4.12). At our best, we realise that we do not yet *fully* hear it right, and thus that God is inviting us on a journey to go on discovering the way Word and life interact. On this journey at times both Word and life appear in a new light and, as a result, we will have to repent and change. The Puritan, John Robinson, put this view in classic form in 1620, when he said, 'For I am verily persuaded the Lord has more truth yet to break forth out of his holy Word.'

This attitude of expectancy and discovery conflicts, however, with that dogmatic Evangelical approach, which all of us have experienced, in which what we find in the Bible is limited to what we already know that it says. Jerram Barrs in his hermeneutical statement wisely calls us to a 'humility before the Word, and a genuine desire to be confronted in our own cultural prejudice and personal pride'. May we all, despite our differences, be of one mind in that affirmation.

John Stott

7. *Reconciling justice and love*

Richard Bauckham and Gordon McConville were very kind to act as hermeneutical arbiters in our 'War and Peace' debate. They were patient in their listening, and skilful in putting their fingers on key issues. Their paper is valuable in identifying areas in which further discussion would be profitable and greater agreement possible. Avoiding simplistic polarisations, they have set an example of the kind of 'map work' (carefully delineating areas of agreement and disagreement) which is needed in all controversy, especially within the body of Christ.

Although they are right to point out that each of the three participants in the debate begins at a different point, with a different text or topic, I am not myself persuaded that the crucial disagreement between us concerns the continuity or discontinuity between the Old and New Testaments. Important as the Old Testament is, the debate between the advocates of pacifism and the just war theory seems to me to be in essence a New Testament debate. It is how to reconcile Jesus' teaching on non-retaliation and Paul's on the State as 'God's servant, an agent of wrath to bring punishment on the wrongdoer' (Rom. 13.4). Pacifists, at least within the Anabaptist tradition, anxious to accord to Jesus a determinitive role, have been uncomfortable with Paul's apparent doctrine of the State. They have tended to explain it away by denying that 'the sword' is a symbol of the authority to take life, and by understanding that Paul reluctantly acquiesced in rather than positively affirmed the State's 'authority' and 'ministry'.

However, I am unable to see this reluctance in Paul. On the contrary, he seems to me to be stating very positively that the State has been 'established' by God with an authority and ministry to promote good and punish evil. If that is so, then the tension is not between Jesus and Paul, but actually within Paul himself. That is, Paul echoes Jesus before going on to describe the duty of the State. He writes both that we should not take revenge and that the State is God's instrument of wrath and vengeance. In this way he speaks of both love and justice.

To sharpen this tension further, we note that Paul writes both of the necessary 'punishment' of evil (Rom. 13.4) and of our duty to 'overcome evil with good' (Rom. 12.21). But how can evil be simultaneously punished and overcome? The only possible Christian answer to this question is to point to the cross. For there God 'demonstrated' (i.e. expressed and revealed) in equal measure his justice and his love (Rom. 3.25, 26; 5.8), condemning evil, in the person of his Son (Rom. 8.3), and thereby overcoming it.

Perhaps in our dialogue about war and peace we have not thought sufficienty about the bearing upon it of the cross. If justice and love, the punishment and conquest of evil, were together revealed in the cross, should we not seek their reconciliation in our attitudes and actions today? We have no liberty to seek to overcome evil by condoning it. That would not be true peace-making, but an unprincipled appeasement. But nor must we insist on the just judgement of evil without any recourse to that divine mercy which mitigates sentences and reclaims offenders. Justice and mercy, judgement and forgiveness, retribution and reform belong together in the cross and therefore in the disciples of the Crucified.

PART THREE

CHRISTIAN

RESPONSIBILITY WITHIN

THE NATION-STATE

Chapter 6

INITIAL REFLECTIONS ON
CHRISTIAN CITIZENSHIP

David Atkinson

1. *The problem of the shape of christian ethics*

In seeking an adequate basis for understanding their responsibilities within the nation-state, Christians have to respond to the fact that there is no one clear tradition of Christian ethical thinking. The problems involved in bringing together the absolute, rigorous teaching of the Sermon on the Mount, for example, and the realities of self-interest and conflict in a fallen world, have led Christians to adopt different approaches to moral decision-making. The problems are compounded by the inherent dilemma of deciding how the view of life shaped by the gospel can be actualised in circumstances very often different from those facing Jesus' first disciples.

Such differences in approach underlie some of the disagreements between Christians on the issues of war and peace. Perhaps the most fundamental disagreement concerns the way Christians should engage with the 'world', and its authorities.

In the Protestant tradition of ethical thinking and action, some Christians (to borrow Nicholas Wolterstorff's terms) take an 'avertive', and others a 'transformative' approach to the world. The first reacts to evil in the world by separation, and by concentrating on building the Christian community into an alternative society or counter-culture. The second confronts evil with a view to change, in the attempt to bring human society nearer to the divine pattern for social order.

Christians in the Anabaptist tradition tend to be more 'avertive'; in the Calvinist tradition, more 'transformative'. Both claim to be biblical. The former tend to derive social ethics from the demands made on the individual by the teaching of Jesus (especially in the Sermon on the Mount). The latter develop their social ethics by inference from a particular approach to biblical theology, concentrating on the implications of the nature of God's justice and peace. The former, out of allegiance to the Prince of Peace, cannot take part in lethally violent actions of resistance against evil. The latter, out of a concern to vindicate God's justice and to fulfil the demands of love for the neighbour, see the waging of war against evil as sometimes a necessary lesser evil.

Martin Luther's doctrine of 'the two kingdoms' was one particular theological approach to the problems. According to Luther, God's kingly rule against the kingdom of darkness is expressed in two modes of government. God rules in the Church through the Word, and in the world through the sword. In the first, God governs through an order in which people make a free response to the gospel of grace. In the second, God governs by ordering society through the magistrate's enforced upholding of civil law. Luther's doctrine separates the Church's authority from that of secular government. It has, however, often been understood as dividing God's work too neatly into two separate spheres in a way that strengthens the fatal divide between private and public morality.

A more satisfactory approach than that of 'the two kingdoms' is one which begins with Paul's teaching about 'the two ages' (cf. Rom. 5.12ff.). (Anders Nygren in his *Commentary on Romans* takes this to be a major key to Paul's understanding of salvation.) Every Christian is caught in the tension of being 'in Christ' as well as still, to some degree, 'in Adam'. We are no longer in the garden of Eden, but nor are we yet in the new heaven and the new earth. We live between the two comings of Christ. God's salvation is already effective but not yet complete.

This means that the world is now related to God in terms of a radical contradiction. God's command to human beings still resembles the command of creation, but it is now accommodated to the needs of a fallen world. We can see this illustrated in the story of God's covenant with Noah. Certain structures within society were instituted to order the life of sinful human beings. The 'orders' (to borrow the Lutheran term) are therefore provisional and temporary. When we speak of God's will we need to distinguish between what is 'perfect' (in the garden) and what is 'provisional' (parts of his law are given because of people's hardness of heart).

There are two main ways in which this important distinction has been rejected in the course of Christian history:

The first possible form is found in the assumption that the radical demands of the Sermon on the Mount . . . are to be proclaimed as the constitutive law of the world, with no regard to the condition of this age. The world is dealt with as though it still existed in its original, created state, or as though the eschaton of the last day had already dawned . . . The other possible way, overlooking the difference between the actual and ultimate will of God, consists in man's transformation of the orders of this age into 'created orders', so that the given circumstances are made sacred, and receive theological legitimacy. Thus war can be understood and sanctified as an ordinance of God. The result is that the intensification of the state, up to and including the totalitarian state and ideological tyranny, is no longer opposed by any theological inhibition. (H. Thielicke, 'The Godless World and the Worldless God', an essay.)

R. Niebuhr is surely right in saying that the kingdom of God is not something that could be progressively realised in history by human action. He is also right in saying that, though all earthly history will be broken by sin, yet human history is not pointless or purposeless. It has a purpose, and it demonstrates important values, but its purpose lies beyond itself.

Because of human sin, there will always be potential or real conflicts in society between individuals and groups. From these conflicts a certain equilibrium of powers will arise, inherently unstable and probably unjust. All human community, therefore, needs organisation. 'Human society . . . requires a conscious control and manipulation of the various equilibria which exist in it. There must be an organising centre within a given field of social vitalities.' (Niebuhr, *The Nature and Destiny of Man*, Vol. II, p. 276.)

Both the provisions of the Noahic covenant with the whole of humanity and an analysis of the human condition in its bias towards the conflict of interests point to the necessity of the

State which God, in his love, has provided as a provisional ordering of a sinful human reality.

2. *The State in the New Testament*

The State in the Gospels is the Jewish State. Jesus made no clear distinction between 'the people of God' and the 'state'. Religion and political life belonged closely together in his day. Nevertheless, Jesus refused to allow that the State's authority had any absolute value. When challenged about the laws concerning sabbath observance, he replied that 'the sabbath was made for man, not man for the sabbath'. He set down a principle that transcends and judges any absolute subservience to the laws of the State. Laws are intended to serve people's needs. 'Politics is for people.'

Jesus' teaching and gestures were such that his mission was misinterpreted as being taken up with national political liberation. As the disciples, travelling on the road to Emmaus phrased it, 'we had hoped that he was the one to redeem Israel'. Jesus, unlike the Zealots, never advocated the overthrow of the governing authority of the moment. Nevertheless, he stood apart and criticised it when it functioned in disregard of God's purposes for human living.

The celebrated phrase, 'give to Caesar what is Caesar's and to God what is God's' may best be interpreted to mean that God claims the whole of life. He reigns supreme, even over the political sphere. There is nothing which belongs to Caesar which does not also belong to God.

At the time of his trial Jesus faced Pilate with the issue of truth (John 18.37). The State has a derived authority, given to it by God (John 19.11). It exists, therefore, by divine permission alone and has a divine commission to fulfil. One of the Church's major responsibilities to the State is to bear witness to the truth: that it is permanently accountable to a higher authority. The State cannot act, therefore, as if it was a law to itself.

Paul in Romans 13 seems to assume a similar framework for understanding the place of the State. All human authority is derived. Civil government is instituted to provide for order and justice and the enhancement of human welfare according to God's purposes ('God's servant for your good'). Negatively, the State exists to serve as God's instrument to judge and punish all wrongdoing.

In spite of the fact that some Christians have interpreted Romans 13 to mean an unconditional obedience to the government in power, it was not written to support blind acceptance of the status quo. Paul's main point is that God has ordered government for the protection of justice, the furtherance of good and the resistance of evil.

By the time Revelation 13 was written (probably in the last decade of the first century) the State had taken on features of ideological tyranny. The beast was granted authority by the dragon (Rev. 13.2), its power rose from the depths of demonic evil. This particular State has exceeded its precise God-given functions and, proclaiming itself a kind of pseudo-church, demands that all people acknowledge its divinity. Here, and in all subsequent despotisms, God's good will has been perverted into vicious idolatry.

3. The State in today's world

It is hard to draw direct lines from the Gospels, Romans or Revelation to Western democracies. Modern sovereign states tend to claim allegience within their own terms, not those laid down by God: yet democracies function by having a constitutionally provided opposition to government.

To decide on a Christian's responsibility within a nation-state today we need to understand who 'controls' power in our democracy and for what ends. In the complex interlocking system which characterises the modern State there are a number of power 'centres': industrial monopolies, the trades unions, education, the media, the civil service, the judiciary, financial institutions which give credit, etc. The duly elected officers of the State, nevertheless, bear ultimate responsibility for governing, and New Testament principles are still highly relevant to their task.

They may know, for example, that the authority vested in government is part of God's purposes for maintaining order within a fallen world. But this authority is never absolute, it is subordinate to God and his laws. The State is therefore responsible to him for how it exercises its authority. It has only a provisional and limited role in the present age. It is God's minister, existing not for its own sake, but to promote and safeguard the welfare of the people, in particular the weak. Governments exist to meet the need for justice. Hence they are responsible to ensure a context of order in which justice (tested in the light of God's justice) can be established. The law and order for which the State is responsible is rooted in the moral character of the creator of all things. The rule of government has to be seen in the light of an order beyond and supreme over itself. All governments should be aware of the danger of separating their authority from the God who has given it. As a result they must exercise power mindful of the temptation to use it in ways that overstep the boundaries set by God. When power becomes highly concentrated and opposition is coerced into silence, government is well on the way to becoming arbitrary, freed in its own mind from any accountability beyond its own decision about what is opportune. Such a government, as Revelation 13 indicates can become demonic.

4. *The modern State and the individual citizen*

The New Testament seems to suggest that it is sometimes right for the State to do what it would be wrong for an individual Christian to do. Christians may not avenge themselves, but the State has a responsibility to enact 'vengeance' on individuals or groups convicted of acting unjustly. The tendency of some Christians, therefore, to insist that the Sermon on the Mount covers both personal and civil relationships will not hold. Paul is clearly moving from an exposition of the Sermon on the Mount in his discussion in Romans 12 about personal relationships to a discussion of a citizen's responsibilities in chapter 13. Different principles operate in each case.

The Christian needs to distinguish his or her responsibilities as a private individual in the realm of personal relationships and his or her official responsibilities as an officer of the State.

The extent to which each individual shares in the task of government is a matter for individual conscience and vocation. But an ethic of neighbour love, which calls us to be concerned not only for our own interests but also those of others, cannot but have social and political dimensions.

The document, *Gaudium et Spes*, from the Second Vatican Council, summarises a Christian's responsibility in this way:

It is fully consonant with human nature that there should be politico-juridical structures providing all citizens without any distinction with ever-improving and effective opportunities to play an active part in the establishment of the juridical foundations of the political community, in the administration of public affairs, in determining the aims and terms of reference of public bodies, and in the election of political leaders. . . . The church praises and esteems those who devote themselves to the public good for the service of men and take upon themselves the burdens of public office.

To say that the State may do what a private individual may not does not mean that the State is outside the rule of morality. On the contrary, the rule of justice, even when the coercive use of force is necessary, can be 'alien' expressions of love. Yet all State law has to be measured by the moral character of God. Both the State and the individual, therefore, are answerable to God and have different responsibilities to perform in appropriately expressing his character. It is part of the Church's responsibility to the State to make clear God's moral rule, and to hold leaders of government responsible to him.

5. *The nation and nationalism*

The seeds of war are often nurtured by an unquestioned ideological commitment to certain sorts of community obligations: e.g. national sovereignty, national honour and national survival. 'Nationhood' is undoubtedly part of the rich diversity of God's world, but is not an absolute. The reality of a *common* humanity under God is more fundamental.

When a nation considers itself sovereign, rather than in submission to the sovereign Lord, and when pride in national membership takes the place of all other identifications, then, as Wolterstorff says, 'legitimate nationalism has become idolatrous nationalism' (op. cit., p. 109). Christians must constantly be aware of a 'nationalism gone cancerous'. Nothing can be so destructive of the *shalom* of God's reign.

No one particular *form* of the State, associated with a particular national identity, can ever be viewed as absolute. What is obligatory for the fallen world is the divine requirements for ordered government. Therefore, for the sake of justice and *shalom*, a particular form of the State may be surrendered rather than risk the outbreak of unjust violence on an international scale.

However, those same moral requirements may sometimes

indicate that coercive force is necessary, as a last resort in a fallen world, to vindicate justice for the sake of *shalom*. And those same moral requirements also severely restrict the means by which justice may be vindicated. Most Christians believe that the *use* of weapons of indiscriminate and disproportionately destructive power (many Christians would include the *threat* of such use) places acquiescence in nuclear war (and nuclear deterrence) outside the bounds of responsible Christian citizenship.

John Gladwin

6. *Links between Church and State*

I have never accepted the proposition that, as a matter of principle, the Church and the State should have no constitutional relationship. This matter can only be resolved by considering, in the light of our faith, what is the right response in any given situation. It is clearly wrong for the Church to be associated with the idolatrous and blasphemous claims of Nazi philosophy. Likewise it cannot be seen to be affirming the atheistic presuppositions of a closed Leninist society. A positive relationship between Church and State cannot thrive when those who control the State seek to use it for ends which are basically hostile to Christian faith. Even here, however, it is legitimate for the Church to claim its place in the life of the nation, whilst remaining implacably opposed to the present order of power. Poland would be a contemporary example of such a situation.

It is worth remembering that four aspects of the political life of any society – the culture, nation, State and government – though related, are quite distinct. They are easily confused, leading some to believe that if the Church has an established position in society it does (or ought to) support the government. The Church may well fulfil its duty to the State by opposing the government. The Church may likewise fulfil its duty to the nation by questioning the form of the State, and it may affirm its contribution to contemporary culture by questioning the attitude and position of the nation.

We also need to consider carefully what we mean by a Church/State relationship. For example, the experience of the 1984 presidential election in the USA is salutory. Here we have a society specifically and formally committed to a clear separation between Church and State, and yet the churches made a profound impact on the election. The greatest pressure was exerted by para-church organisations like Moral Majority. The formal leadership of the main-line churches, in general, took a different political line. In some respects the Church in the USA is an integral part of the nation, believing it has a role to play in influencing the form and life of the State.

We need, therefore, to distinguish carefully between a formal Church/State arrangement and what actually happens. The formal situation, as either the Church or the State perceive it, may not coincide at all closely with what actually happens in real life. The Church in Poland, for example, is excluded from the political organisation of the Polish State. It remains, however, very powerful in political life and seeks to influence events. The Church of England, on the other hand, although it is included in the political organisation of the British State, may have much less power than its Polish counterpart.

7. *The reality of modern Church and State*

I want to identify some aspects of the present situation in Europe in general and in the United Kingdom in particular which affect our judgement on the appropriate form of the relationship between the Church and the State today. Firstly, Christendom has declined and a plural and secular society has grown, and in some respects taken its place. In our pluralist society the State has a duty to all citizens, a proportion of whom affirm no allegiance to any religious institution and practice, whilst others belong to a variety of different religious traditions. In our secular society religious considerations rarely influence the actions of the State directly.

Secondly, the Church has ceased to be the collective voice of the nation gathered together as a religious community. Even established churches have increasingly become one denomination among others. Although the Church carries a faith which is not sectarian, because it embraces the whole of life and experience, it is supported by only a part of the community which owes some allegience to the State. Along with other organisations, therefore, it strives for the mind of the community.

Thirdly, the inheritance of the past leaves tensions in the

present situation. In pastoral matters the church has duties which have their origin in a Christendom past, e.g. the requirement to perform civil marriage for any (with the exception of divorcees) who may call on its services. In the public areas, when the Church is taking a greater active interest in matters of political concern (such as the nation's deprived communities), some MPs may wish to return to a situation where Parliament directly orders the internal affairs of the Church. There are signs of some reluctance on both sides to accept the nature of the changed context in which we live.

Fourthly, the modern State is a very different body from that which existed in past eras. Today it is large and powerful and creates large expectations in the community. It commands extensive resources and takes an interest in ever-widening circles of community life. The twentieth century has witnessed not only the development of ideological States – be they Marxist, Nazi, Islamic, or of any other kind – but also the growth of state power and organisation everywhere. The State employs vast numbers of people, controls considerable wealth, sets the boundaries of citizenship, provides services, organises defence on a permanent basis and is involved in myriads of ways in the everyday life of citizens. Can the Church create any effective relationship with a body as diverse and amorphous as this?

Fifthly, the modern Church is itself a pluralist body. It is made up of many groups no longer under one universal or national umbrella. When we talk about the relationship of the Church to the State, what church are we talking about?

8. *Questions still to be resolved*

We can only begin to formulate the nature of the relationship between Church and State today when we have thought hard and long about a number of central questions. There is the issue, for example, of pluralism in both Church and State. Is it possible to find shared values which enable a sense of community to be built across diverse cultural and other boundaries? There is the issue of the modern State as we know it. What responsibilities does it have, and what are its limits? What is the citizen's duty towards it? What role does the Church have today in the local and national community? What limits are there to its mission in society? What set of responsibilities do the kind of churches and states which exist owe to one another? What models of Church/State relationships are compatible with Christian faith? And, finally, how should both the Church and the State work towards establishing better kinds of relationship?

Donald Shell

9. The modern nation-state

A prerequisite for our discussion is to think carefully about the nature of the collective organisation, the nation-state. The term is widely used, though only roughly accurate. In the context of a discussion about war and peace, we are really dealing with the State, or as lawyers would say 'sovereign States'. In this sense the State has invaded every part of the globe (even Antartica and the Oceans). It is 'sovereign' in a technical sense both in terms of breadth (within a defined territory) and in terms of depth (i.e. the State can do what it wills with its own).

To arrive at satisfactory ethical decisions from a biblical perspective, there is a sense in which we have no option but to take the world as we find it. But the problem when we adopt such an approach is how to take whatever principles we believe Scripture affirms about government (e.g. the responsibilities of rulers) and apply them to the governments of sovereign States. We need, then, to begin by thinking critically about the modern reality of the State from the standpoint of the Bible.

All sorts of mystical ideas about 'the State' have proliferated throughout history. Frequently notions of temporal power have in practice been checked by notions of spiritual power, at least in the minds of those involved. The situation today, however, has radically altered: now in much of the world the 'spiritual powers' no longer constitute a realistic check, and this at the very time when the potential for the temporal power to develop 'depth sovereignty' is greater than ever before. Totalitarianism properly understood is a twentieth-century phenomenon, and there is an incipient or latent totalitarianism about all modern States.

For these reasons we need to develop a theology which enables us to appraise the very notion of 'sovereign States', before we begin to think about our responsibilities within them. In doing this we might especially consider the following issues which relate to the way States operate in the contemporary world.

Firstly, to what extent is society a much more fundamental concept than that of the State? There are many different human societies, in part evidence of the variety a loving Creator built into creation, in part evidence of divisions resulting from human sinfulness. We have responsibilities to our neighbours, and this includes in some senses all those human societies of which we are part – from our street to our workplace to 'Western society' and 'human society' in the widest sense. Responsibilities to these societies must be set alongside responsibilities to the 'State'. At times they may conflict quite sharply (e.g. in the case of support for human rights).

Secondly, to what extent has the State assumed an unhealthy dominance in our thinking? In an important sense the State is no more than one level of government, and government is one aspect of society. Governments exist at various levels – wherever a recognisably distinct society exists. In the modern world attention has been focused on the State to such an extent that it becomes sacrosanct. People supporting both left- and right-wing ideologies have fallen into the trap of reifying the State. A mythology about the role and importance of the State has resulted.

Thirdly, to what extent in real political terms is not the title 'sovereign State' a seriously misleading misnomer? Much of the time, talk of 'independent sovereign States' is a smokescreen to hide ugly facts about exploitation, dependency and repression. To interfere in the internal affairs of another State is conventionally considered most indecent. Hence, though everyone is doing it, no one can openly admit that it is a legitimate action in some circumstances. Furthermore, there is a basic unreality about using the same term to cover both the USA (with almost a quarter of the world's GNP) or the USSR (with a sixth of the world's land mass and a dozen nationalities), and most of the one hundred and sixty or so other States in the world today.

Fourthly, the existence of a level of 'government' beyond the level of the State calls for more emphasis. Bodies such as the UN, EC, OAS, ASEAN, have governmental responsibilities. In international law State sovereignty typically means such bodies have little standing. How does a biblically based theology of government regard them? They are the governmental expressions of recognisable human societies, with increasing importance, I would suggest, beyond that generally accorded to them today. Likewise a theology of government would point towards the need for regional, local, sub-state government to receive greater emphasis than typically is the case.

Emphasising our membership of human societies, each of which has government as an aspect of its existence, before that of a State, affords a different perspective on our relative responsibilities to each. There is obviously a need for a balance between the two, but in our day the State receives a disproportionate attention. This then becomes a damaging distortion when the question of the use of force arises.

10. Government and the use of force

Government is a feature of human society approved by God for the purpose of establishing and maintaining justice. The prime responsibility of government is to ensure as far as possible that the structures of society result in fairness between individuals and groups. In some circumstances, at least, government has the responsibility to use force. While the New Testament does not speak directly of the responsibilities of rulers (presumably because, though early Christians were husbands, wives, children, slaves, masters and subjects, they were not rulers) it does speak of rulers' task, as God's ministers, to punish wrong and reward right behaviour.

In particular rulers have a responsibility to use force to execute God's wrath on wrong-doers. This means that rulers have a duty, in those circumstances where it is unavoidable, to harm people physically. It is quite a distinctive task. Jesus' teaching in the Sermon on the Mount about turning the other cheek is reiterated by Paul, significantly in the passage immediately prior to his description of the responsibility of rulers. That teaching is normative for all Christians in their personal relationships. It is an ethic of non-resistance to evil, and as such goes much further than the pacifist normally wants to go.

The danger in using teaching of non-resistance in the context of collective organisations, especially governments, is that we lose sight of the extreme sharpness of this teaching for us in our personal relationships. The ethic of non-resistance in such relationships is where Christian peace-making should start. If Christians were genuinely obedient there, who knows what the spreading consequences of such obedience might be? But it is wrong to apply this teaching about one-to-one relationships to situations where whole communities are involved.

In using force to resist evil, rulers must act justly. Within a state that particular action involves seeking to maintain a peace based on justice by eradicating or limiting the causes of strife. Between governments similar considerations apply. At this level, however, rulers have to consider with particular care whether or not to use violence to resist evil. In certain circumstances, at least, rulers have a responsibility to use violence to protect their subjects, for this may be the only way to sustain a just rule within the community for which they are responsible. It is the government's duty to protect the legitimate interests of those for whom it is responsible, not its own interests as such.

There is a certain ambiguity about violence throughout the Scriptures. On the one hand, violence has a hopelessness and futility about it, which understandably leads some Christians to eschew it entirely (a 'priestly' pacifism). On the other hand, the fact that violence is an inevitable feature of human life, and is sometimes necessary to lessen evil, also seems to be recognised.

The just war doctrine is an interesting attempt to systematise scriptural teaching on the subject. But it is fundamentally artificial, academic and unreal. In so far as it encourages prudent thought about the use of force and instils a cautionary attitude, it is helpful. But it hardly captures the reality (the spirit of dynamism) of biblical teaching about the conditions of war. The main problems with the just war doctrine are that its propositions are not operational, and it almost certainly encourages self-delusion. For a country ever to go to war is an awesome decision. People are always killed and maimed in war, whether by bows and arrows or nuclear weapons. The outcome of war is never certain, and usually not predictable. Combatants and non-combatants alike suffer.

11. The nuclear factor

There are dangers in over-emphasising either the continuities or discontinuities between 'conventional' and 'nuclear' war. Nuclear weapons should make us think much more carefully about *any* kind of war (and indeed have done so). Even taking into consideration the destruction involved, there are important continuities, for the total destruction of whole communities is not a feature of nuclear war alone.

The discontinuities in general receive much more emphasis. One crucial point is that nuclear weapons inevitably require a strategy for any future war different from those of the past. Indeed every technological advance in the methods of waging war has required new thinking about strategy. To fail to do this is both simple lack of prudence and, in the case of nuclear weapons, gross neglect of responsibility. The argument cannot therefore be simply about whether or not nuclear disarmament should take place, but how, given the existence of such weapons, disputes between States should be conducted. This takes us from the immediate response of war to the conduct of diplomacy.

It is here that assumptions about sovereign States must be challenged. The problem over nuclear weapons cannot be resolved in isolation. In practical terms it is just as necessary (and just as difficult) to change current attitudes to the State, as to bring about a renunciation of nuclear weapons.

The statesman's task in recognising where the path to justice lies is desperately hard. However, too much political leadership at every level seems to be much more reactive than creative. A pattern of leadership in which leaders are willing to be driven from office, if they cannot achieve a fundamental goal they have set themselves, needs to be re-established.

Good leadership is often a question of recognising when the time is ripe to mobilise opinions on some issue, and then perceiving how to do this. The politician takes principles and applies them to empirical reality. Sometimes an important principle cannot be applied for the time being. The validity of the principle is not thereby denied; it is simply set aside until some other activity has run its course. Furthermore, while Christians should stir up opinion by declaring principles, we also need to recognise that the method and timing of putting such principles into effect lies primarily with the politician.

In closing, a couple of brief examples might help us to understand the relationship of principles and practice. Supposing the British Prime Minister is convinced that the renunciation of nuclear weapons by the UK would destabilise the Western Alliance and increase in a measurable and significant way the likelihood of conventional war in Europe, then I think it would be wrong to disarm unilaterally. Or supposing an American

President, by making an issue of human rights questions in the USSR, angers Soviet leaders (who interpret his actions as intolerable interference in their affairs) and thus provokes a negative and uncooperative response on disarmament negotiations, then he has acted foolishly. Such examples remind us that beneath all the outward bluster, good statesmanship is ultimately a matter of making knife-edge judgements in areas of ethical conflict.

President, by making an issue of human rights questions in the USSR, angers Soviet leaders (who interpret his actions as intolerable interference in their affairs) and thus provokes a negative and uncooperative response on disarmament negotiations, then he has acted foolishly. Such examples remind us that beneath all the outward bluster, good statesmanship is ultimately a matter of making knife-edge judgements in areas of ethical conflict.

Chapter Seven

ISSUES RAISED FOR CHRISTIANS BY THE MODERN NATION-STATE

Andrew Kirk, editor

1. Deciding where to begin

In the centuries-old debate between Christian pacifists and Christians who believe that the lethal use of force in some circumstances is God's will, one of the major causes of dissent concerns the theological starting-point adopted: it may be God's sovereignty (Reformed); justification (Lutheran); the redeemed community (Anabaptist); the two kingdoms (Lutheran and Evangelical pietism). The starting-point can easily become both the point of reference and the controlling factor. It acts as a 'canon' within the Canon which determines how the rest of Scripture is to be read. Are we justified in giving any one facet of salvation history a privileged position? How do we use one aspect of biblical teaching to organise the whole into a coherent unit without thereby neglecting other aspects?

Another way of stating the same case is by saying that Christians differ from one another in the amount of emphasis they give to the great moments of God's self-revelation: creation, the fall and God's judgement on it, redemption and the consummation of all things at Christ's second coming. There is a danger of working from fixed theological positions with inflexible theological models. The understanding of the fall and its consequences is a good example. Just as in the economic sphere, the fall has been used to defend both free-enterprise capitalism and a centrally-planned economy, so with this issue it has been seen as conclusive proof both for the limited use of force in certain circumstances of conflict between nations and for the renunciation of all force in international relationships. Owing to this ambivalence, there is a clear case for one Christian to listen to *how* another is using the particular doctrine in question and to point out what aspects of it may have been neglected.

2. *Choosing between hermeneutical keys*

We do not think 'the two kingdom' approach to Christian ethical decision making, as classically expounded in terms either of law and grace or of fixed sovereign spheres, is a helpful way of looking at Christian civil responsibility. It suggests that God presents two different faces to the world. It also tends to separate moral responsibility too rigidly into the personal and private sphere of life and the corporate and public one. Historically it has tended to produce a 'quietist' (no change) attitude on the part of Christians toward government policies and the use of power. It is hard to see how the prophetic dimension of Christian ministry could be theologically justified using its criteria.

However, we do favour another approach which superficially might look similar – that of 'the two ages' (cf. Luke 16.8; Rom. 12.2; 1 Cor. 2.6; Eph. 1.21; Tit. 2.12; Heb. 6.5). The primary difference between the two resides in their relationship to salvation history. The theory of the two kingdoms appears to separate the realm of God's salvific work too sharply from the realm of his judgement and coercive power through the State. This results in a static view of law and order, which easily degenerates into an uncritical acceptance of any given historical moment. The two ages, on the other hand, points to two realms, or ways of living, which overlap in the present. In this case the impact of the age of salvation is felt within the existing order. Having a more clearly defined eschatological orientation than that provided by the view of the two kingdoms, the perception of the reality of two ages provokes a perpetually critical response to political power. The difference between the two approaches in discovering God's work in the world has led to a strong division of opinion among Christians about the kind of stance they ought to adopt towards the public sphere of life.

Though we believe that the notion of the two ages is a more clearly enunciated biblical concept it does not easily solve all problems of political involvement. A sharp tension between the first fruits of salvation and the full harvest of redemption still has to be worked through. Christians simultaneously live out the reality of the groaning of the whole creation in its suffering and the hope of the liberation of the children of God (Rom. 8.18ff.).

On the one hand, Christians have to take into account the evidence all around them of a disastrously distorted and corrupted order. From God's Word they know that this is the result of idolatry and injustice (Rom. 1.18), made worse by human beings' arrogant pretence to be wiser than God himself (Rom. 1.22–3). On the other hand, they also know that God's final response to wickedness is to take upon himself, in the Son, the full consequences of sin, liberating and transforming those who recognise that in the historical events of the death and resurrection of Jesus is the solution to all forms of evil. There-fore they lift their heads high, expecting to see the effects of salvation breaking into the present world. In the light of the resurrection of Jesus Christ they are not permitted to take a cynical view about the possibility of change.

The balance in the tension between pessimism and utopi-anism has been called 'realism'. This may be a helpful term, if defined in a way consistent with the whole of Christian teaching. It must be biblical realism, not the timid prudence of 'realpolitik'. To reiterate too facilely that 'politics is the art of the possible' is to beg the question in God's world as to what is possible.

3. Belonging simultaneously to two kinds of world

The approach from the side of the two ages raises another question, which has also produced different responses among Christians: how does a Christian express his responsibility as a citizen of two different realities? Probably the Christian pacifist/ non-pacifist divide finds its clearest focus at this point. The former conclude, from their study of Scripture, that their God-given calling is to bear witness to the coming age of reconcili-ation and peace. In so far as they are able, the whole of their lives must be consistent with this witness ('. . . as far as it depends on you, live at peace with everyone'). That use of force which involves ending another person's life clearly is not compatible with that witness, and therefore represents a betrayal of the gospel which speaks of the reality of a wholly new life in Christ. The pacifist's testimony is to the future reign of God, already making its impact on this world. Faithful discipleship, in declaring in visible form the values of this new age, entails the willingness ultimately to sacrifice one's own life rather than to have to sacrifice someone else's.

The latter argue, from an equal attention to Scripture, that this approach tries to resolve the tension between evil and righteousness before God's final intervention. Christians are called to live responsibly within an unjust world and to seek to implement justice whenever possible. The struggle for justice may on occasions involve Christians in sanctioning and using force to restrain the growth of evil. The non-pacifist testimony is to responsible human decision-making in the present, in order that God's will may be more perfectly fulfilled in society before the end.

Are these two positions irreconcilable? Is there, perhaps, a fundamental difference about ends as well as an obvious discrepancy about means? Clearly, discussion has resulted in different approaches to practical action. The consistent view of the pacifist can be summed up in the *title* of a book by J. H. Yoder, *Christian Witness to the State* (Newton, Kansas, Faith and Life Press, 1964). The non-pacifist would prefer to speak of 'Christian witness within the State'.

4. Acting responsibly in the world

Yoder in his article argues that the burden of proof is on those who believe a Christian has a duty to participate in the responsible use of political power. He bases his position on the apparent abstention from political life of both the apostolic and sub-apostolic Church and the generally recognised disaster of the accord between the Church and the State initiated by Constantine. In particular, he makes much of the documented evidence that Christians in the first three centuries did not take up arms. Either the willingness or the refusal to fight to defend the State is often taken as the touchstone of involvement in

political life, it being argued that those who refuse to kill cannot
be serious about the exercise of power.

Non-pacifists argue on the other hand, that refusal to take up
arms was for the early Church a matter principally of emperor-
worship.[2] In situations, like those of Western, democratic
nations, where the State and its authorities are no longer
invested with divine attributes, this reason no longer applies.
Moreover, they would contend that the pacifist does not do
justice to the need to reinterpret Christian obedience according
to changed historical circumstances. The situation of the early
Church in the Roman Empire, as that of a persecuted and
despised minority, is only one model of Church–State relationships. The pacifist-anabaptist view of society has never come
to terms with the possibility that the Church, because of its
numerical strength or moral influence, may inevitably be a
factor of power. In South Africa, for example, where some
ninety per cent of the population are practising Christians, how
could Christians abstain from exercising power at different
levels of society?

Moreover, the non-pacifist, in a further response to the pacifist, would say that the burden of proof falls on the latter
to demonstrate that all Christian involvement in political life
necessarily entails the kind of compromise that happened
following Constantine.

In many ways this particular aspect of the debate may be
more theoretical than real. In actual life the pacifist does seek,
if not to utilise power for his own cause, at least to bend it in
his direction. Demonstrations, vigils, the refusal to pay taxes,
the lobbying of Parliament are not exercises in non-power, but
in the use of power by other means.

Likewise the self-critical non-pacifist does not allow the ends
to justify the means in every circumstance. There are different
degrees of conscientious objection. And Christians, therefore,
who are committed to political involvement must be ready to
resign, if their principles are compromised. They may have to
withdraw for a time in order to bear witness. Such action,
however, does not foreclose later re-engagement.

5. Dividing ethics between a private and public realm?

We are not convinced that maintaining a tight distinction
between a personal and a collective practice of love is a helpful

way of approaching the question of the use of force. The usual resort to the distinction between Romans 12 and 13, and to the Sermon on the Mount as representing only the 'heroic' ethic of personal relationships, does not do justice to the whole context of these passages.

We recognise that the closer one moves to limiting an issue to personal ethics the more one is inclined to arrive at an absolute ethic (e.g. in the case of abortion). However, in the case of war and deterrence it is usually the non-pacifist who insists that the pacifist's case is built on an illegitimate leap from an absolute personal ethic to the public arena. On the other hand, pacifists do not necessarily accept that the Sermon on the Mount is only concerned about personal discipleship in a private sphere of life (that would be an easy caricature of their beliefs). Nor do they accept that in reality such a separation is either legitimate or possible.

A neat division between the personal and the collective can lead to the dangerous conclusion that, in given circumstances, the individual can suspend his or her moral judgement and hide behind corporate decision-making. This has happened, and is likely to happen, in the prosecution of war, as individuals become caught up in the emotional fervour of a cause which is made to seem right and legitimate by one-sided propaganda and discrimination in the use of the facts. A fairly recent example of this might be the Commons debate which immediately preceded the sending of the Task Force to the Falklands (April, 1982), and the subsequent sinking of the Argentine cruiser, Belgrano.

People can only act ethically if they can be held responsible for what they do. In the case of a supposedly corporate act of love who is accountable for what and on what grounds? Nevertheless, in spite of difficulties, it might be said that the example of the persistent witness of Bishop Bell of Chichester during the 1939–45 war against certain methods adopted in the Allied implementation of the war, demonstrates that Christians can maintain a critical atitude even within a collectively-prosecuted, fundamentally just, moral cause.

6. Implementing justice across national boundaries?

We have not made great strides forward in the debate about the just use of force across national boundaries. We believe that one point which needs further reflection is the fundamental rationale for force in the just war tradition. Some Christians incline strongly to the Augustinian view that Christians have a responsibility to vindicate justice against evil. This conviction may involve a nation in taking the initiative in prosecuting hostilities in order to end a situation of gross abuse against another people. Other Christians take Aquinas' position that force is legitimate only in cases where the defence of citizens against unprovoked aggression from outside a nation becomes unavoidable.

Declaring war against Hitler in 1939 might have been justified on either view: response to the Nazis' 'final solution' or defence of the territorial integrity of Poland. In both cases, however, the nation going to war has to act as counsel, judge and jury in its own case, deciding in its own cause and according to its own interests that the balance of the right and the good is on its side. This is a procedure which, of course, would be entirely illegitimate in any normal judicial procedure. It is equivalent to a government imprisoning and punishing civilians, without allowing them a trial in which to plead their own cause and cross-examine the case against them.

The non-pacifist would argue that, because normal standards of law within a nation obviously cannot be applied in practice between nations, the gravity of particular situations demands actions which cannot be ruled to be wrong just because there may be anomalies in the events leading up to war. This reasoning is based on the necessity of having to choose in real life between the lesser of two evils. To do nothing is to allow one course of evil action to triumph.

The pacifist would counter that, even laying aside theoretical considerations of principle, war is always the greater of two evils because of the inevitable consequences which flow from it. In the actual event of war those engaged in it tend to sweep under the carpet its negative effects, or else always to stress that the balance of good (the ends) outweighs the unfortunate (but inevitable and necessary) evils (the means). The pacifist does not accept that the use of force can be neatly divided in this way, for he believes that in real life the means also seriously affect the ends, which in the process of war easily degenerate into something considerably less noble than the original high aims.

7. *Living with the modern State*

We agree that there are a cluster of important issues which surround notions of nationhood and sovereignty. The contemporary world has given birth to the nation-state as a self-contained entity, organised as a unitary whole within prescribed geographical boundaries. Nothing quite like it existed in biblical times.

It may be possible to draw a distinction between nation, State and government. The first represents the history and identity of a people with defined cultures and linguistic codes. The third is a given group of people who at any one time operate political decision-making power within a nation. This group has usually adopted a coherent political philosophy or ideology. The second is more difficult to define, but probably is to be located in the continuing structures which form the executive arm of central government (the civil service, government departments, etc.).

Modern nations are inconceivable without a State apparatus, for the diversification of modern life, growth in the economy, the sophistication of technology, the heightening of people's consumer aspirations and the greater degree of political participation have all led to the expansion and proliferation of bureaucracy. It is basically this second aspect of our modern societies which has no real parallel in Scripture, unless one is inclined to interpret it in the light of Paul's references to the principalities and powers.

If the distinction between nation, State and government is valid, it may be that the Christian has a varied calling in relation to each. It is, however, the State which causes us the greatest misgivings. The reason is basically that it appears to be an entity simultaneously autonomous from effective democratic control, unaccountable in many of its operations (e.g. its secret service) and remote from ordinary citizens. It tends naturally to drift both towards tightening control over the lives of members of the community and requiring an increasing, albeit ill-defined, allegiance to its way of operating.

The drift of the modern nation-state towards an ever more centralised structure of power can be seen most clearly in our generation in the creeping recourse to the doctrine of national security as a reason for suspending natural justice, politicising the police forces and withholding information from the public.

It is not without significance that the ideology of the national-security State has arisen in many parts of the world within the last twenty-five years. It has invariably been accompanied by a restriction on civil liberties, the loss of human rights and the arbitrary use of force. There is a sense in which this ideology may be a natural partner of the growth of State bureaucracy.

National security is undoubtedly a basic factor in the debate about deterrence. And yet, considerable doubt must surround the whole concept. It is ill-defined and therefore can become stretched like a piece of elastic in the hands of any government. The celebrated case at GCHQ, Cheltenham (1981), of the right to belong to a Trades Union, or not, has displayed how an (abstract) idea can take precedence over natural justice. It might well be apposite to ask whether national security does not often really mean State security or even the protection of government from investigation, from imagined real or potential opposition or from ideologies which the established power does not like. In many cases it becomes a reason for restricting the working of an open society. Unless a public debate on the meaning of security is initiated, ordinary citizens have a right to be suspicious that the concept is being manipulated in the interests of one sector of the population.

Lesslie Newbigin in his book, *The Other Side of 1984*, argues that in our irreligious culture the State has taken the place of God. He points out that, whereas in a time when a Christian view of the world held sway, blasphemy used to be the most serious crime, today it is treason. Treason only makes sense in the context of a duty to render absolute loyalty to the State. Such homage must come close to what Christians rightly call idolatry. Treason is the betrayal of a given system of power; it is a subversion of the existing order of things. Though not to be undertaken capriciously, when it seems to be the only recourse for the sake of justice, the protection of the rights of minorities or to avoid a massive programme of militarisation, treason cannot be considered an absolute moral wrong. Some of those accused of treason in the past (Jeremiah, Bonhoeffer, Luwum) are today heroes in the Christian portrait gallery.

What we are saying is that what the State regards as treason may in certain clearly defined circumstances be the only kind of check against the encroachment of an unreformable, centralised power (known technically as 'depth sovereignty'). It is a kind of ultimate way of calling attention to the deformation of the

State as it starts down the slippery slope towards acting like the 'beast'.

8. *Approaching the interpretation and application of the Bible*

Finally we have sought to address the thorny question of biblical hermeneutics. We can only record a few points which seem to us important as we wrestle with the contemporary meaning of the biblical message.

i. We have already drawn attention to the danger of over-playing any one biblical concept as the starting-point and determining grid for all subsequent debate.

ii. Reading the Scripture in the light of our situation involves more than careful exegesis of individual texts. It calls for a process of theological reflection which begins with a thematic study of the whole of the Bible and engages with those questions from our context which we believe need to be addressed in a special way. Exegesis (which is highly rated in the British empirical tradition) is a necessary check on theological reasoning at those points where the Scriptures are being specifically used to substantiate particular conclusions. As an isolated exercise, however, it is of limited help in determining ethical stances.

iii. In the overall context of this particular debate we suggest that the following might be a helpful way into the text:
(a) case studies (such as Ellul does in his *Politics of God and the Politics of Man*) of figures like Joseph, Jeremiah, Daniel and Pilate);
(b) an investigation into the intention of the law;
(c) an exploration of the specific aspects of God's nature as these are demonstrated in particular historical situations (e.g. the Exodus, the institution of the monarchy, the Exile and Restoration, in Jesus' relationship to authority and in the Book of Revelation).

iv. One of the differences between the Old and New Testaments is that the former addresses God's people as 'citizens', whilst in the latter they are 'subjects' in a wider world context. In a formal way we in Britain are both. However, because of historical development, we are given responsibilities in society (e.g. those which accompany the right to vote) unparalleled in biblical times.

v. The tested way of moving from the general theological

principles of Scripture to the specific reality of our own world is through middle-axioms and paradigms. A *middle-axiom* can be described as a general policy statement derived from a universally valid postulate. Thus one can move, for example, in a natural progression from God's non-discriminating love to the upholding of justice to the demand for the redistribution of wealth to a progressive tax-system. The middle-axiom in the sequence would be the redistribution of wealth. A *paradigm* is an example or model from one historical situation which corresponds substantially to an event in our times. The search for relevant paradigms might cause one, for example, to discern the values which spring from Israel's political and economic constitution and ask what is their contemporary reference-point. A paradigm forces us to ask about the relation of principles to the concrete form they take in a given situation. To what extent, for example, is the value being upheld separable from the specific expression in which it is framed in the Bible?

vi. The conclusions about Christian thought and obedience today, achieved through the kind of deductive or extrapolative approach we have been hinting at, may be tested by viewing them in the light of the four cardinal doctrines of Christian faith: creation, the fall, redemption in Christ and the consummation of all things (for an example of this method, cf. Andrew Kirk, 'Race, Caste, Class and the Bible', *Themelios*, Vol. 10 No. 1, January 1985).

vii. The hermeneutical task, because it involves asking the type of questions of the biblical text to which it cannot respond directly, has an element of ambiguity about it. This is compounded by the finiteness of our individual perspectives and propensity to be selective in what we are prepared to hear. A limited degree of plurality within the Church may express more faithfulness in our witness to Christ than a hasty consensus. Might this be one conclusion we have to make from the protracted debate between pacifists and non-pacifists? Or, is there fresh understanding of God's will to be uncovered which could help those with strong convictions on both sides to move closer together?

We are convinced of the need for biblical Christians to develop exceptional clarity and integrity of thought in this area, to continue to listen with the utmost attention to one another in spite of the passions which are engendered, and to pray together for the process of discussion to be genuinely shaped by the Spirit of truth and holiness.

Note

1. Pacifists dispute that this was the primary motive. They would claim that both many Christian theologians and church disciplines forbade the taking of life in any circumstances.

Chapter Eight

RESPONSES TO THE

DIALOGUE

Richard Bauckham

1. War against the State

It is surprising, perhaps, to find that the question of a just war in relation to the modern nation-state is raised only as the question of war *on behalf of* the State, and not also as the question of armed resistance or revolution *against* the State. But the latter is the really significant issue for Christians in many parts of the world today (and even arises within the United Kingdom, in Northern Ireland). Thus, for example, South Africa is mentioned in Chapter 7 as an example of a country where Christians cannot avoid taking positions of power in the State. But for many South African Christians (who, being black, are in any case not eligible even to vote, let alone hold office in the State) the real question is whether it could ever be right to take up arms against the State.

This is of great relevance to the points of difference and convergence between pacifists and non-pacifists in the arguments of Chapter 6. In one sense, the tendency to relativise the authority of the State represents a movement from a traditional, 'conservative' non-pacifist position (concerned with the legitimacy of Christian participation in the wars of nation-state against nation-state) towards a concern in which pacifist and non-pacifist may agree: namely, that the Christian cannot owe absolute loyalty to the State. However, for the Christian non-pacifist, the logic of this tendency may well, in certain circumstances, lead to the legitimacy of participating in revolutionary movements. The more pacifists, for their part, have moved from a position of political non-involvement to one of participation in active, but non-violent, resistance to bad government and illegitimate State power, the more they may sympathise. Not the central point of disagreement will emerge again in a different form.

2. *Loyalty to one's nation*

I wonder whether it should be 'the State which causes us the greatest misgivings'. The concerns which are then expressed are valid and important, but I wonder whether they are not a response to a relatively easy question, by comparison with the more difficult question of the Christian's loyalty to the *nation*. The need to protect civil liberties and to relativise State authority is reasonably widely recognised in Western nations at present, but to suggest that one's loyalty to one's *nation* – the particular people to which one belongs – must also be relativised will meet deeper and, in a way, more legitimate feelings of disquiet. After all, people may well feel absolute loyalty to the State only because they do not distinguish it from absolute loyalty to the nation.

The status of the nation as a value for which one may kill is of as much relevance to political violence in the contemporary world as is the question of loyalty to the State. Should Christians criticise the IRA simply for killing the innocent, or should they also condemn this organisation's idolatrous attitude to Irish nationhood as a value for which any sacrifice is justified? Criticism of *State* idolatry is more pertinent to a critique of Soviet militarism than to that of American militarism. The problem in the latter case is that a nation with an admirable record in recent years of limiting *State* power internally in the interests of civil liberties and an open society, also possesses (according to its many critics) an aggressive sense of absolute right to pursue externally its *national* self-interest.

Questions of the degree of right and value attaching to such things as national self-determination and even national survival are difficult ones for Christians. Arguably, the Church in the West has not yet fully recovered from its degeneration, since the late Middle Ages, into separate national churches with the correspondingly tenuous sense of its international character.

But to the extent that it does, the resulting tension between the Christian's national and international loyalties can be fruitfully made explicit in the interests of a distinctively Christian contribution to the political sphere. Hermeneutically, the proper relationship between the nationalism of the Old Testament and the international perspective of New Testament Christianity needs exploring.

3. Correcting partisan interpretations

In the hermeneutical task it is important to recognise the influence not only of the kind of starting-points mentioned in Part I, but also of the political context and political concerns out of which biblical interpretation comes. This is particularly relevant because, all too frequently, biblical interpretation has served, unconsciously rather than cynically as a kind of religious justification for political self-interest. The only effective remedy for this kind of bias is to listen to how the Bible sounds to Christians in quite different political, social and economic circumstances from one's own. Of special value, for our present concerns, is the way in which Christians who are the victims of political violence of various kinds, read the text for themselves.

Gordon McConville

4. The possibility of agreements in general and in detail

Two main points, out of those which the authors of Chapter 7 agreed on, stand out: the ambiguity inherent in a Christian's living in two worlds, and the possibility that political involvement can produce change for the better, even though the whole creation 'groans' in its expectation of a greater kind of liberation. Such difficulties as the need to affirm 'a collective practice of love', in spite of the danger of being seduced by jingoism, and the need to register effective protest when the State arrogates too much power to itself, are also clearly identified. The question of the degree to which agreement can be attained is recognised by the fact that Christian pacifists and non-pacifists do not necessarily occupy antithetical positions concerning the Christian's relation to the State, but they seek to bring influence to bear in their own ways. Differences are understandable when one recognises that the Bible does not clearly indicate how one should participate in political processes. Hence Christians cannot agree about explicit, clear-cut answers to the difficult questions of decision-making they face in day-to-day life, though they may concur about general goals and attitudes.

The authors of Chapter 7 have set out (particularly in section 8) *preliminary* guidelines for a more detailed study of the biblical text. I would underline both the need for a dialectic between exegesis and theological reflection and the recognition that the Bible provides paradigms (via 'middle-axioms') for Christian action. The structure provided by the four doctrines – creation, fall, redemption in Christ and consummation – is also important.

5. Concerning starting-points

Nevertheless, there are areas – where, from the point of view of biblical hermeneutics, I feel some unease. First, though the idea of two ages is powerful, its adoption as a hermeneutical key represents rather too narrow an exegetical base. The relationship between the ages is not simply one of the imperfect waiting for the revelation of the perfect. Titus 2.12 probably comes closest to that idea, while Ephesians 1.21 is an important statement of the lordship of Christ over both ages. Other passages, however, set the two ages more firmly at odds with each other: we are delivered 'from the present evil age' (Gal. 1.4); the wisdom of God is 'not a wisdom of this age or of the rulers of this age' (1 Cor. 2.6); ' . . . the god of this age has blinded the minds of the unbelievers . . . ' (2 Cor. 4.4). In the New Testament, then, the two-age structure of reality is typically used to highlight the moral and spiritual struggle in which the Christian is involved. This must imply that the two-age structure is not in and by itself a mandate for political action.

The second point follows from the first: the two-age idea does not put the discussion in a wide enough context. The choice of this key arguably fails to meet the authors' own correct requirement that theological reflection should be on the broadest possible canvas. The biblical basis advocated comes entirely from the New Testament. For this reason, other criteria of interpretation (such as the structure of creation, fall, redemption and consummation, also identified in Chapter 7) are not given sufficient weight. Alongside the radical discontinuity suggested by the idea of the two ages, that structure allows certain continuities to emerge: e.g. the essentially 'political' nature of humanity and the fact that the consummation of God's action for salvation will be fulfiled in a 'new heaven and a new earth'.

From these general observations about the hermeneutical starting-point, let me go on to focus on two other aspects of the argument which also provoke in me certain reservations. The first is the distinction which is proposed between nation, State and government. This seems to me to multiply problems. Could there be a loyalty appropriate to the *nation* in the abstract, if that notion did not correspond to any specific political entity or even ran counter to political realities? Such loyalty would be no more than an anachronism, or hopeless aspiration. At best, it is only obliquely related to the question before us. More importantly, direct biblical authority for the suggested analysis of the political entity, the nation, seems to be lacking. I do not mean that the Bible says nothing much about this, only leaving us to work out our own positions on the basis of general ground-rules. I mean rather that the Bible does have things to say about the nature of political endeavour which render the proposed analysis dubious.

Crucially, the Bible gives, I believe, a mandate to govern. This I find in the commission to humanity in Genesis 1.28 to '. . . have dominion over . . . every living thing that moves upon the earth'. Government, then, to borrow the terminology of Genesis 1, is in itself a 'good' activity. This perspective comes from our understanding of God's act of creation. The Bible then goes on to give us numerous instances of actual government, most of which in practice are far from 'good'. History abundantly demonstrates reality from the perspective of the 'fall'. This perspective continues to have relevance in our modern, 'fallen', world. In common with all other aspects of living, however, the 'good' and 'bad' aspects of government are held together. As human beings we are involved in both, whether we like it or not. This is why the great political figures of the Bible (e.g. Joseph, Jeremiah, Daniel and Mordecai) are prepared to be actively involved in States whose view of government is invariably self-serving despotism. Here is the heart of the Christian's ambiguous position: governments are more or less bad, but the activity of government is good. According to our biblical examples, the godly people are likely to float to the top.

Because these biblical examples are paradigms which constitute attempts (whatever their own perspectives on the matter) to fulfil the biblical mandate, it is hard to sustain a negative judgement on the State as opposed to the government. There can be no government without machinery. In actual governments 'king' and 'court' (to keep the biblical categories) need each other to fulfil the mandate to govern. When God's people clash with the ruling powers, a distinction between these is not an issue. Daniel and other political leaders insert themselves into the whole system with a minimum of fuss. I agree with the observations made about the tendency of modern government to become more and more removed from ordinary citizens, and that secrecy and the growth of an impersonal bureaucracy show an unacceptable face of government. But, in the tendency to hedge government about with appeals to national security, there is not always a significant distinction made between attitudes of the government of the day and bureaucracy. The example used (GCHQ) is surely a case in point. Implied in this discussion is the assumption that the biblical categories have their counterparts in modern situations.

The second point, where I am not in full agreement, concerns the way in which the Christian actually participates in the processes of government. If the point made in the foregoing paragraph holds true, the Christian, participating in the normal processes of political life, cannot remain aloof from using means to achieve ends. Some Christians, having seen at close quarters how legitimate ends (e.g. the defence of Western democracies against the aggressive expansionism of an atheistic and totalitarian empire) are secured by means they regard as immoral, have chosen not to associate themselves with those means. I am not sure that this supreme difficulty for those who advocate participation has been fully explored in the statement of Chapter 7.

One cannot idealistically serve the party which seems to offer the most acceptable defence policy, pretending that the infrastructure which will service that or any other policy will be wholly enlghtened. There is a problem with the statement that Christians who are committed to political involvement must be ready to resign, if their principles are compromised. Though self-evidently true in one way, it nevertheless masks an unavoidable hard fact, namely that in public life, almost by definition, the Christian's principles are *always* compromised. There is something slightly luxurious about the thought that it will always be possible to resign if Christian principles are offended. This is because, even in modern democracies, culturally influenced by the Christian tradition, at bottom the controlling spirit is not Christian but at best utilitarian. In opting to participate in the exercise of power, Christians have to come to terms with this fundamental fact. This conclusion does not in any way deny or question the duty to keep up specifically Christian pressure on governments and government agencies. Exercising pressure, of course, does not necessarily imply the rejection of participation. The sort of activity attributed to Bishop Bell of Chichester can be engaged in by both those who advocate active participation and those who do not.

Though a full-blooded participationist position looks decidedly tenuous, our biblical examples will help to give a rounded perspective. There was little conspicuously 'Christian' about the States that Joseph, Daniel and other Christian leaders served. Yet, in their involvement it is hard to think what would have constituted a matter calling for resignation. Mordecai, for example, took on the 'premiership' in Persia while a decree of genocide remained in force against his own Jewish people. Where some Old Testament political figures ceased exercising their functions (Daniel, for example), it is because the State, in its idolatrous requirements, had ceased to find *them* acceptable. I do not think this means that a Christian should never resign. Resignation is a weapon which has meaning in our societies, and as such it is available for our use. However, as a weapon, it is itself part of the process of participation. The value of the Old Testament examples is that they furnish models which enable us to face the most acute difficulties which participation presents to the Christian. At the same time, the theological context in which they come enables us to understand what participating in the political process truly involves.

This discussion might appear to raise the question of the status of the Old Testament as the most difficult hermeneutical problem. Without attempting to resolve this issue in detail, I have tried to offer a way in which the task of taking the witness of the whole Bible seriously might be pursued.[1]

Note

1. I have developed the approach advocated here more fully in 'Christian Participation: a Biblical View', *Evangel* 4 (1986), pp. 15–18.

PART FOUR

TOWARDS A CONSENSUS?

Chapter Nine

SUMMING UP

Ernest Lucas

Having got so far in this book, some readers may be disappointed. After a lengthy process of dialogue, a group of Christian scholars, all professedly accepting the Bible as their authority, have failed to reach a wholly common mind on one of the pressing issues of the day.

Jerram Barrs is still convinced that:

We are responsible in our moment of history so to value the principles of justice and the need to resist and restrain evil that we should be prepared to maintain whatever deterrent force is necessary. To abandon deterrents would not produce peace but might bring even greater injustice on earth. (p. 17).

Here 'deterrents' includes a nuclear first-strike capability.
For Alan Kreider, the fact which is determinative is that in the Sermon on the Mount:

Jesus, then, calls his disciples unconditionally to respond with love (not killing) to the one enemy whom his nation was tempted to resist by collective violence (p. 24).

This means that Christians should not participate in war or any other form of violence.

John Stott, however, concludes that:

The State may use force, but only discrimininately. . . . The force permitted to the State does not extend to the shedding of innocent blood. Therefore, the Christian conscience, which has been schooled by Scripture, must condemn every use of force by the State which is uncontrolled or indiscriminate. (p. 44).

Hence in war, there must be no indiscriminate use of conventional weapons, nor any use of indiscriminate weapons, namely atomic, biological and chemical weapons.

There are areas of overlap between these three positions, but there is not consensus. As I have said, this will disappoint some.

The failure of Christians to agree must always be a genuine cause of disappointment. However, I would ask those who are disappointed, 'Is the real cause of your disappointment failure to reach a *consensus* or the failure of *your* view to carry the day?' A major achievement of this book and the process it records is the demonstration that Christians can disagree over an important issue in a way that is open, honest, respectful and eirenic. The key to this is that one can sense in the writing (and I know personally this reflects the attitudes of the people involved) that there is no desire to defend a party line or to be proved right. Rather, there is a common concern to discover, as Alan Kreider puts it, how the Word of God and life interact, and a willingness to let the Word confront cultural prejudice, personal pride, and received traditions in the process. This, as he says, is the only way to avoid limiting what we find in the Bible to what we already 'know' that it says. This dialogue provides a model that is worthy of being copied by others facing other issues.

Realistically, one could hardly expect that a disagreement which has lasted for centuries, during which both sides have refined their arguments in support of their positions, could easily and speedily be resolved. One could, however, reasonably expect that the strengths and weaknesses of each position might be clarified and that the roots of the disagreement might be exposed.

Andrew Kirk points out in his introduction that the disagreement between Jerram Barrs, Alan Kreider and John Scott can be traced to two roots: differences in the way they use the Bible to derive ethical guidelines, and differences over the relationship between State, the Christian, and the Church. Parts II and III of the book pick up these issues. Here, I want to comment on the strengths and weaknesses of the three positions, as I see them. I ought first to reveal my own position. I did not take part in the process which resulted in the book, and I came to reading the manuscript with a position similar to that held by John Stott. That I did so, was the result of working for about three years in the Merseyside Churches Peace Concerns Group. Reading the manuscript caused me to reconsider my view, without, however, resulting in any radical change in it. Nevertheless, the fact that I came to the manuscript with formed views has not, I hope, prevented me from appreciating the strengths and weaknesses of each position. So, what are they?

For me, a major weakness in Alan Kreider's case is his treatment of Romans 13:1–6. I agree wholeheartedly with his plea that we should aim to understand the historical setting of the passage in order to appreciate how it would have been understood by its first readers. He makes a good case for the view that they would have seen in it a challenge to put aside insubordinate behaviour in the face of an oppressive regime. However, he fails to take a proper account of the point made by John Stott, that what Paul says *to Christians* is based on what he says *about rulers*. The teaching about rulers is brief, but seminal, and its implications need to be drawn out and faced. Alan himself asks the question, 'Who is the proper instrument of God's punitive justice?' (p. 30). I am sure that the New Testament answer is, the rulers, whose office is ordained by God. There is, it seems to me, nothing in the Bible to indicate that Christians should steer clear of involvement in government office, and some which implies that they should get involved. This being so, I think that the distinction made by applying Matthew 5:43–8 and Romans 12:14–21 to the personal behaviour of Christians, and Romans 13:1–6 to what they may do if acting as officers of the State is necessary, valied and coherent.

The strength of the pacifist position is that it takes seriously the radical nature of Jesus' ethical teaching, which requires that his followers live differently from the world around them. Alan Kreider is right to say: 'We must not, however, be less concerned than Jesus was that our salt might "lose its savour". Much Christian participation in the structures of our society, it seems to me, has been so compromised ethically as to make no specifically Christian contribution' (p. 32).

To be involved in the life of the world and yet to live differently is to live with tension. It is all too tempting to seek to avoid this either by becoming uninvolved (a temptation for the pacifist) or by conforming to the world (a danger for the non-pacifist). Alan's call for imaginative, unconventional forms of involvement which express Christian values could provide a basis for *practical* co-operation between pacifists and non-pacifists without requiring either to compromise their ethical stance.

One weakness I see in Jerram Barrs' position and which I wish to highlight is that the use of nuclear weapons is incompatible with the responsibility given to humans to care for and develop the earth as God's stewards. Jerram argues that nuclear weapons are not qualitatively different from all other weapons. I beg to disagree. One major difference is their abilty to render large areas of territory uninhabitable for decades by people, animals and even possibly plants, as a result of radioactive fallout. The Chernobyl catastrophe gives a small indication of what might be on an infinitely larger scale. (It is possible that some chemical and biological weapons could have a similar effect on the environment. This, plus their indiscriminate nature, puts them in the same moral category as nuclear weapons.) To this, of course, one can add the 'nuclear winter' effect of a major nuclear exchange. I could not, as a Christian, contemplate the use of weapons which would so despoil what God has created. This argument is not meant to *replace* the argument based on shedding innocent blood, but to add to it a dimension that was only touched on in the dialogue process (p. 64).

For me, the strongest and most attractive aspect of both Jerram's and John Stott's argument is their insistence that justice and love are not opposites, but must go together since both are concerned with how people relate to one another. Jerram is right to point out that, whilst strict pacifism can be applied quite readily when I am relating to a neighbour who is threatening me, its application is not so obvious when I am faced with a powerful neighbour threatening the life of a powerless one. To whom do I show love, and how, when the aggressor refuses to listen to reason and disarm? One might say, with due reverence, that in the Old Testament we sometimes see God faced with this dilemma when Israel was oppressed by her enemies.

On such occasions, we read of God as the warrior fighting for and with his people. In fact, God is mentioned in direct or indirect relationship to war in all but three of the Old Testament books – the books of Ruth, Esther and The Song of Songs. I cannot dismiss such references as a result of a 'primitive' concept of God which Christians could and should abandon. To do so has serious repercussions on one's understanding and doctrine of Scripture. Rather, I see in them a truth about how God *acts*, rather than what God *is*. They do not show God to be a militarist approving of war, but that he acts in the world *as it is*, through *sinful* human beings, to achieve a greater measure of justice and peace than there was before. This means at times that he supports his people when they can do no better than opt for the way that involves the *least* evil.

Sometimes, this meant participation in a war in order to prevent a greater injustice and to establish a measure of peace. If God has been willing to get involved in this way, risking misunderstanding and the impugning of his moral nature, should we not be ready to do so too?

Richard Bauckham and Gordon McConville point out what is for me a serious weakness in John Stott's position. This is his attempt to justify the possession of weapons, the use of which he regards as immoral. As they say (p. 65), the possession of a deterrent is meaningless unless there is the intention of using it. To pretend a willingness to use it, is to act deceitfully, and so immorally. Hence, possession of a deterrent without the willingness to use it is either pointless or immoral. Whilst I differ from John at this point, I share his 'Christian realism' which seeks to work from the situation *as it now is*.

We are in a moral mess because we (the UK/NATO/the West) do possess nuclear weapons. Nuclear pacifists wish we did not. The obvious way out might seem to be unilateral nuclear disarmament. However, there may be moral and immoral, or at least more moral and less moral, ways out of an immoral situation. I share John's concern that immediate unilateral nuclear disarmament might make nuclear war more likely, rather than remove the threat of it. The Christian doctrine of human fallenness suggests that we need to be prudent. Fallen human beings are given to such things as the opportunistic exploitation of such advantages as having superior power. Hence, I find myself drawn to support a policy of balanced, multilateral and verifiable nuclear disarmament. Within the context of such a policy, there is room to take unilateral steps towards disarmament as a means of indicating good faith and gaining the other side's confidence.

I do not intend to say much about the discussion in Part III of this book. Here, there is a high degree of consensus, as Chapter 7 shows. All I want to do is support Gordon McConville's caution about the use of the two ages idea as a hermeneutical key (p. 115). It is a valuable and powerful one but must not be made an exclusive key. It does tend to make the exegete blind to the Old Testament material that might be relevant to the issue. There are two reasons for this. The first is that the two ages language and concept is drawn from the New Testament, and so those who use it tend to have their attention fixed on the New Testament alone. It might help here to recognise that one root of the two ages concept is to be found in the Old Testament teaching about the age of peace/salvation that will be ushered in by the Day of the Lord. Secondly, the emphasis on the two ages idea is on discontinuity, and the tendency is to assume that the Old Testament speaks only about the old age. This makes it seem irrelevant to the Christian who is already experiencing something of the new age. Here there is a false assumption about the Old Testament which arises from a wider problem of the relationship between the two Testaments and how we should use the Old Testament as Christian Scripture. The problem is not a simple one but it must not be avoided. There is room here for more work to be done on the right use of the Old Testament when seeking to think Christianly about moral, social and political issues.

I will close with a further word to those who are disappointed about the failure of this project to produce an evangelical Christian consensus on the problems of war and peace. Might it not be that we are wrong to expect such a consensus in a fallen world? We are in a moral mess and it may be that there is no simple way of sorting it out. Moreover, as is pointed out more than once in this book, the problem of understanding and applying the Bible is due in part to differences in the interpreters' historical, cultural, personal and ecclesiastical setting. To this we must add the fact that in our finitude, not to mention our fallenness, we cannot expect to see things with the clarity and wholeness that God does. Our vision of reality is bound to be partial and so distorted. As a result, it may be that on some complex moral issues Christian witness has to take the form of different groups offering their differing insights and challenging each other, as well as the non-Christian world, to deeper thought and self-examination. If that *is* the case, then

it is vitally important that Christians do not spend their time
and efforts in heated verbal battle with each other, so vitiating
their witness to non-Christians, but live in honest and eirenical
dialogue with each other, never giving up the search for closer
agreement, but not becoming disheartened if the search appears
to be a long and hard one. Part of the reason for the existence
of both the London Institute for Contemporary Christianity
and the Shaftesbury Project is to initiate, encourage and sustain
such dialogue on a variety of contemporary issues, of which
war and peace is only one.

Roy McCloughry

I am sure that the reader will by now sympathise with my wish
not to dwell on the substantive issues of war and peace
contained in the debate as these have been ably discussed in
the preceding chapters. My small contribution is to make some
comment on the process by which such a debate comes about
and what our expectations of it should be.

The Christian faith is not a bundle of esoteric statements
about 'issues' or even about 'doctrine'. It is the totality of what
happens when God interrupts us and transforms our lives.
Theology cannot therefore be divorced from the Christian
community. It is not of course subject to it else it could not
effectively provide the necessary stimulus to prevent the
Church's tendency to become preoccupied with itself. But
where theology becomes dry, aloof and autonomous it must be
called back to serve the believing community. When it loses
its nerve under the pressure of secularism or any time-bound
ideology, it must be encouraged to recover its authority. Always
and everywhere, theology should inform the mind, strengthen
resolve and encourage the heart, equipping us to build up the
body of Christ 'until we all attain to the unity of the faith and
of the knowledge of the son of God.' (Eph. 4:13)

An alarm bell should therefore ring when theologies appear
to compete with one another. It may be that one theologian
is overemphasising one aspect of a situation while another
underemphasises the same point. It may be that each is drawing
attention to one aspect of an eternal truth which is expressed
in a doctrinal tension such as the sovereignty of God and the
'free will' of man. It may be that one is right and the other is

wrong. But if they contradict one another they cannot both be right. In sorting out the muddle we will find that intellectual differences are not the only ones at stake, nor will they always be the most important ones. Differences in style, personality, background, politics or even emotional make-up may influence the most carefully prepared debate detrimentally.

Certainly those of us who took part in the 'live' consultations represented by this book became aware that it was not enough to read the papers meticulously prepared by Jerram Barrs, Alan Kreider and John Stott. To truly understand them in context one had to try to understand the people who had written them. Alan Kreider's pacifist stance was not developed in a library surrounded by books. It is a reflection of the way in which God has led the whole of his life to this point. It is an essential part of his pilgrimage and of the way he expresses his faith in God.

Part of the excitement of doing theology is that insofar as it is committed thinking for a committed community[1] it is possible to disagree with another's point of view while deriving great richness from their own experience. One of the most revealing things that happened over the course of the years that separated these events, was the way in which those most involved in the debate grew to understand and respect one another.

It may be then that the phrase *The Christian Mind* which has recently come into vogue, should be replaced or at least complemented with an emphasis on *The Christian Heart* as the seat of not only our thought processes but also our emotional response to God. The heart is the place where the intellect and the emotions are integrated. The former phrase, though useful in reasserting the fact that our minds matter in an age when Christians are awash with feelings and a lack of commitment to the public sphere, does emphasise the cerebral and the abstract. This is not to say that we should return to the spiritual wastelands of the privatised and possessive individualism of past decades ('you in your small corner and I in mine'), but reinstate the idea that we respond as whole human beings to God, history and even ideas. Christian thinking is not an abstract and academic exercise. It is a necessary (if not sufficient) part of our response to God's revelation of himself

---

[1]cf. **Stepping Stones** (ed. Christina Baxter) (Hodder and Stoughton 1987), p. 17.

and his claims on our lives, both as individuals and as a community.

However, it is not enough that we experience the Holy Spirit of unity while contradicting one another, as he is the Spirit of Truth. Nor is it enough that each protagonist is an accurate reflection of his or her tradition as if we were all consumers choosing a point of view but needing reassurance of the quality of the goods on view. Pluralism is good insofar as it represents the freedom to think one's own thoughts under God. It is a statement of fact in that it describes the world as it is. In the same way as political compromise is not a statement of intention to display moral weakness so much as a description of the world as those who practise politics find it, so hermeneutical pluralism is an admission of differences, divisions and deviations. In the evangelical world with its background of monism, such an admission usually provides the motivation for a movement towards consensus. We are uncomfortable with anything which does not suggest that all the pieces of the jigsaw have been laid on the table for us and all we have to do is find out how to put them together.

Those with neat minds might find it offensive that three people who disagreed on such an important issue should still disagree after so much time and effort has been put into (presumably) getting them to agree. But as I have intimated above, there was much more to the process than a succession of statements. The value of this volume is that it records a dynamic historical process rather than a single statement which purports to act as a benchmark against which to test our beleifs. There is no easy way of learning from this process. Each person who has reached the last pages of this book (without cheating!) has had to weigh the arguments, work with the scriptures and work towards a greater understanding on this very complex set of issues.

The fact is that each participant did not remain isolated in his tradition surrounded by those who agreed with him. Each participant was willing to expose his position to those who would be most critical of it. In doing this they demonstrated a willingness to have their views tested by a critical audience and took it on faith that it would also be a supportive community. This is encouraging because on issues where Christians disagree with one another, there is all too often a willingness to knock down straw men. The opposition case is put weakly, or with some obvious fatal flaws which the 'insightful' Christian analyst then proceeds to demolish. Such Pyrrhic victories do nothing to convince the onlooker that Christians are actually concerned for the truth.

The Christian is called to understand how a fellow Christian can hold a high view of scripture, be equally concerned with hermeneutics as he or she is, and yet hold views diametrically opposed to their own. Only when they can argue the opposition case as if it were their own with no hairline cracks in the argument can they be sure that any subsequent victory for their own argument has a claim to also be a victory for the truth. Such a strategy not only relies on a truly humble mind but also on an unshakable belief that there is such a thing as revealed truth and that the Holy Spirit is the only sure guide to its whereabouts. Such an attitude has more to do with wisdom than with the tawdry accumulation and decumulation of knowledge which passes for it in much of the modern world.

In the practice of politics and economics some of us long for equality. We know that it will not come in an absolute form. We may be honest enough to admit that if, by some miracle or sleight of hand, it were thrust on us from the heavens it would no sooner arrive than it would be corrupted by mankind's innate wilfulness and unending quest for self-gratification. The fact that it will not come may be a cause of despair for honest but time-bound ideologues. It is however only a greater spur to those who know that one day justice will be done and demonstrably so. Equality may not be realisable but a greater degree of equality than exists at present is certainly something worth fighting for.

The same is true of the quest for truth. Christians are called to hope and not fatalism. The search for truth might also be the cause of much perplexity but for those who long for the darkened glass to clear through which all of history and therefore eternity is now viewed, it can never be the subject of a hopeless despair. We move towards it. True, the steps we take may be small, but they are all necessary.

All longing for the truth to be revealed clearly and in its entirety is a longing for the kingdom of God to come. The kingdom is already among us and in Christ we have been set free by the coming of the truth. For Christians the gospel and the Christ of the gospel is an oasis of certainty perceived with the eye of faith. In other areas we are myopic, now blinded by prejudice, now ill informed, now preoccupied with other priorities in our busy lives. Advance is correspondingly slow. To claim that we have the answer in an area in which it is patently clear that we do not, is very dangerous. We live in an age ravaged by the presentation of uncertainty, doubt and cynicism as evidences of human maturity. This cancer has left a generation hungry for certainties. There are those who call themselves prophets who will always peddle in false security. The calling of the Biblical Christian is to proclaim clearly what God has proclaimed clearly and to work with integrity with others at those things which are less clear. Those who long for a single truth which unites all in the quest for world peace, and also in a common method of obtaining it, will call the outcome of these consultations a failure. By their standard, it is of course a failure. But Christianity is called to influence history from within and that requires an understanding of the limits of human knowledge. Without such an understanding we may be tempted to despair ourselves when Christians disagree. The debate represented here is a record of disagreement but it is both constructive and instructive. When disagreement between Christians becomes destructive we can be sure that there is disobedience at its root.

There are many social, economic and political issues which cannot be solved through exposition alone. The various points of view on offer are so bound up with human history and culture that social analysis is needed before it even becomes clear which questions of principle it is important to ask of scripture. In these cases it is not only important to draw on the training of social scientists, but also to realise that those who came as theologians to offer their gifts will also have been affected by this process. It may be some time before a hermeneutical community becomes aware that its position on an issue such as nuclear deterrence has been more affected by the culture of patriotism, nationalism or reactions against them than by scripture, even though one's position is expressed through scripture. The dawning of such a realisation and the subsequent willingness to lay all prejudice down openly is the beginning of maturity.

It is important then that the interpretation of scripture on complex social issues is not only cross-disciplinary but that it is genuinely cross-cultural. It is also vital that we look long and hard at the sociology of knowledge, that is the social process by which people arrive at their conclusions. All this assumes a committed human community in which mutual disclosure can take place without defensiveness. This is 'speaking the truth in love', which is the way in which 'we are to grow up in every way into him who is the head, into Christ.' (Eph 4:15)

In the early twentieth century it was scientific statements which were regarded as having absolute authority. Words like 'fact' and 'proof' had an objective quality which was distinctly reassuring. The idea that the authority of science, based as it is on rationalism and observation, could be questioned was anathema. In the enlightenment the scientific paradigm had replaced the theological precisely because nature was open to observation in a way that spiritual life was not. Sir Karl Popper was the one of the first to insist that scientific theories are never verifiable only falsifiable, then his successor Imre Lakatos said that even this was not possible and that scientific theories were a collection of competing research programmes, some of which just fall away because they do not seem to be going anywhere. The American, Thomas Kuhn, then dispensed with truth altogether and saw science as a socially defined enterprise; the boredom of normal research, a humdrum activity, punctuated by infrequent orgies of revolution. Finally Paul Feyerabend ridiculed the idea of scientific method and introduced a permissive ideology of 'anything goes'.

This is important to us because one gets the feeling that some of those Christians who take part in debates such as this one on social issues hanker after just that degree of authority which could belong to scientific endeavour only when it was abstracted from the lives of the scientists who were involved with it. Science has had exactly the same problem as theology with the interpretation of the data. Nature, is still a given, the problem comes with its interpretation because at that point human endeavour in the form of the observer and the scientific community, is drawn into the picture. Similarly the authority of scripture is a given among evangelicals, but any problems are compounded when we attempt to interpret and apply it relevantly to modern life, drawing together the culture of scripture and contemporary culture to provide a coherent and cohesive picture. It is not that this is not possible, indeed it is essential that we succeed, it is just that we need to learn from what has happened to our colleagues in the scientific community. It is not enough to say that they have succumbed to the spirit of the age and mourn the passing of their authority. We must learn from the realism that has now invaded their ivory towers of abstraction. All human statements are touched by provisionality, we cannot escape from this. What we can do is believe that we are not alone, but are aided by the Holy Spirit who is leading us into all truth. It is not true for theologians that 'anything goes' since the divine revelation contained in the scriptures is a 'given'. However it remains true that many Christians are worried by hermeneutical pluralism believing that we have become too accustomed to accommodating it and do not let it spur us on to exploring one another's positions. They rightly believe that pluralism can not only provide an opportunity but also an embarrassment which may divert the church from its true task.

If we are to advance as a Christian community in our penetration of the secular world, and if we are to provide a model of 'unity in diversity' in a world in which differences lead to divisions which lead to deviations, then reading one another's books and writing reviews on them is not enough. It is important that we constantly seek to draw together those who naturally disagree and foster relationships between those who do not understand one another. In others words the business of academic advance and intellectual rigour when conducted within the body of Christ, is irrevocably tied to the practice of loving our brothers and sisters. Fellowship, the sharing of resources, is the right context for wisdom to flourish and those who become entrenched in a position which is open to challenge by the rest of the Christian community but resist attempts to being drawn into that community in order to open up dialogue may rightly come to be regarded as mavericks by others.

Both the Shaftesbury Project and the London Institute for Contemporary Christianity who sponsored these consultations seek to foster just such a forum for debate. We see these consultations as a first step rather than the last word, but they are definitely a step forward not only in the substantive content of the conclusions but in the way things were done.

BIBLIOGRAPHY

Albrecht and Koshy, *Before it's too Late: The Challenge of Nuclear Disarmament*. Geneva, WCC, 1983.

Barclay (ed.), *Pacifism and War*. Leicester, IVP, 1984.

Barrs, *Peace and Justice in the Nuclear Age: Christians and Pacifism*. Greatham, Garamond Press, 1983.

Cameron, 'The Christian and Nuclear Weapons' in J. Stott (ed.), *The Year 2,000*. Basingstoke, Marshall Pickering, 1983.

Davis (ed.), *Ethics and Defence: Power and Responsibility in the Nuclear Age*. Oxford, Blackwell, 1986.

Kreider, 'Nuclear weaponry and Pacifism' in J. Stott (ed.). *The Year 2000*. Basingstoke, Marshall Pickering, 1983.

Mills-Powell, *Decide for Peace: Evangelicals and the Bomb*. Basingstoke, Marshall Pickering, 1986.

Stott, 'The Nuclear Threat' in *Issues Facing Christians Today*. Basingstoke, Marshall Pickering, 1984.

Wolterstorff, *Until Justice and Peace Embrace*. Grand Rapids, Eerdmans, 1983.

Yoder, *Nevertheless: The Varieties of Religious Pacifism*. Scottdale, Herald Press, 1971.

Yoder, *The Original Revolution: Essays in Christian Pacifism*. Scottdale, Herald Press, 1971.

Yoder, *The Politics of Jesus*. Grand Rapids, Eerdmans, 1972.

INDEX OF BIBLICAL REFERENCES